Be Distinct

WARREN W. WIERSBE

While this book is intended for the reader's personal enjoyment and profit, it is also designed for group study. Study questions are located at the end of the text.

Run So That You May Win
ivictor.com

Victor is an imprint of
Cook Communications Ministries, Colorado Springs, Colorado 80918
Cook Communications, Paris, Ontario
Kingsway Communications, Eastbourne, England

BE DISTINCT

First Printing, 2002
Printed in the United States of America

  2 3 4 5 6 7 8 9 10 Printing/Year 05 04 03

Sr. Editor: Craig Bubeck
Cover Design: iDesign, Etc.
Cover Photo: Artville
Study Questions: Sue Moroney

Library of Congress Cataloging-in-Publication Data

Wiersbe, Warren W.
  Be distinct : (2 Kings) / by Warren W. Wiersbe.
    p. cm.
  ISBN 0-7814-3303-7
  1. Bible. O.T. Kings, 2nd--Criticism, interpretation, etc. I. Title.
  BS1335.52 .W53 2002
  222'.5407--dc21
                                        2002001083

C O N T E N T S

PREFACE

"The Christian life is not a way out of life but a way through life," said evangelist Billy Graham. God doesn't save us and hide us away until He takes us to heaven. He saves us and then drops us into the midst of difficult situations and challenges, and He expects us to make a difference. According to Romans 12:1-2, if we surrender to the world around us, we become conformers; but if we yield to the Holy Spirit and dare to be different, we become transformers and God uses us to accomplish His will.

The book of 2 Kings describes what happens to a people when the conformers take over. It records the end of the northern kingdom of Samaria when the Assyrians took over and the captivity of the southern kingdom of Judah by the Babylonians.[1] Both kingdoms rebelled against the covenant of the Lord and became like the idolatrous nations around them. Many of the kings of Judah followed the example of Jeroboam and Ahab, not the example of David. God sent His people messengers to call them back to the Word of God, men like Elijah and Elisha, as well as kings like Jehoash, Hezekiah, and Josiah. "But they mocked the messengers of God, and despised his words, and misused his prophets, until the wrath of the Lord arose against his people, till there was no remedy" (2 Chron. 36:16).

When society around us is in moral and spiritual darkness, God's people need to be lights, and when society is decaying because of sin, we need to be salt. *We must be distinctive!* Paul calls us to be "children of God without fault in the midst of a crooked and perverse generation" (Phil. 2:15, NKJV). "If a man does not keep pace with his companions," wrote Henry David Thoreau in the conclusion to *Walden*, "perhaps it is because he hears a different drummer. Let him step to the music he hears, however measured or far away."

The hour has come for God's people to be alert to the voice of God and obedient to the will of God—to be distinctive. God is seeking transformers, not conformers.

Warren W. Wiersbe

A Suggested Outline of 2 Kings

Theme: God's judgment of Israel and Judah

I. The ministry of Elisha (2 Kings 1–13)

II. The fall of Samaria (2 Kings 14–17)

III. The captivity of Judah (2 Kings 18–25)

ONE

The Parting of the Ways

Elisha ("my God saves") had been Elijah's servant and apprentice for probably ten years, but now time had come for the Lord to call His courageous servant home. We get the impression that they were men with different dispositions, Elijah being the "son of thunder" and Elisha the gracious healer. This doesn't mean that Elijah was never tender or that Elisha was never stern, for the biblical record shows otherwise. But in general, Elijah came like John the Baptist, putting the ax to the root of the trees, while Elisha followed with a quiet ministry like that of Jesus (see Matt. 3:1-12 and 11:16-19). In the closing events of this spiritual partnership, we see revealed four important truths about the God of Israel.

God judges sin (2 Kings 1:1-18)
After the death of wicked King Ahab, the nation of Moab took advantage of Ahaziah, his son and successor, and broke the bonds of vassalage that had chained them to Israel (v. 1; see 3:4-5). Years before, David had defeated Moab (2 Sam. 8:2) and Ahaziah's successor Jehoram (Joram) would join with Jehoshaphat, king of Judah, to fight against the Moabites (3:6ff). But the Lord is in charge of the nations of the earth (Acts 17:24-

28; Dan. 5:19, 21; 7:27), and His decrees determine history Ahaziah was an evil man (1 Kings 22:10, 51-53), but when the Lord isn't allowed to rule, He overrules (Ps. 33:10-11).

Idolatry (vv. 2-4). A decade or so before Ahaziah's accident, Elijah had won his great victory over Baal (1 Kings 18), but Ahab and Jezebel hadn't been convinced or converted and neither had their family (1 Kings 22:51-53). When Ahaziah was severely injured by falling through a lattice, he turned for guidance to Baal and not to the Lord God of Israel. "Baal" simply means "lord," and "Baal-Zebul" means "Baal is prince." But the devout remnant in Israel, who worshiped Jehovah, made changes in that name and ridiculed the false god of their neighbors. "Baal-Zebel" means "lord of the dung," and "Baal-Zebub means "lord of the flies," one of the names His enemies used to insult Jesus (Matt. 10:25).

Why did the king decide to send messengers forty miles away to Ekron to consult the priests of Baal? True, Elijah had slain the 450 prophets of Baal (1 Kings 18:19, 22, 40), but that was ten years ago. Surely other priests of Baal were available in the land. The king's parents had fed hundreds of these priests at their table (1 Kings 18:19), and it wouldn't have been difficult for King Ahaziah to import priests of Baal to serve as court chaplains. Perhaps he sent to Ekron for help because he didn't want the people in Samaria to know how serious his condition was. The temple of Baal at Ekron was very famous, for Baal was the chief god of that city, and one would expect a king to send there for help. Note that Ahaziah asked the priests of Baal for a prognosis and not for healing.

God keeps His servants informed about matters that other people know nothing about (John 15:15, Amos 3:7). This "angel of the Lord" could well have been our Lord Jesus Christ in one of His preincarnate appearances (Gen. 16:7;18; 21:17; 22:11; 48:16). When God's servants are walking with their Lord, they can be confident of His directions when they need them. This had certainly been Elijah's experience (see v. 15 and 1 Kings 17:3, 9; 18:1; 21:18). Elijah intercepted the royal envoys and gave them a message that would both rebuke and sober the king. Why did he want to consult the dead god of Ekron when the living God of Israel was available to tell him what would happen? He would surely die! This ominous declaration was made three times during this event—twice by Elijah (vv. 4 and 16) and once by the messengers (v. 6). Instead of being spokesmen for Baal, the messengers became heralds of God's Word to the king!

Pride (vv. 5-12). It seems incredible that the king's messengers didn't know who Elijah was and didn't learn his identity until they returned to the palace! Elijah was Ahab's enemy (1 Kings 21:20) and Ahaziah was Ahab's son, so certainly Ahaziah had said something to his courtiers about the prophet. The description the messengers gave of Elijah reminds us of John the Baptist who ministered "in the spirit and the power of Elijah" (Luke 1:17; Matt. 3:4). The phrase "a hairy man" (KJV) suggests his garment rather than his appearance. The NIV reads "with a garment of hair." Like John the Baptist, Elijah wore the simple camel's hair garment of the poor and not the rich robe of a king (Matt. 11:7-10).

The announcement that he would die should have moved Ahaziah to repent of his sins and seek the Lord, but instead, he tried to lay hands on the prophet. (This reminds us of King Herod's seizure of John the Baptist; Matt. 14:1-12.) Ahaziah knew that Elijah was a formidable foe, so he sent a captain with fifty soldiers to bring him to the palace; but he underestimated the prophet's power. Did Ahaziah think that he could kill the prophet and thereby nullify the prophecy? (The Lord's words in v. 15 suggest that murder was in the king's mind.) Or perhaps the king hoped to influence Elijah to change the prophecy. But Elijah took his orders from the King of kings and not from earthly kings, especially a king who was an idolater and the son of murderers. Years before, Elijah ran away in fear when he received Jezebel's threat (1 Kings 19), but this time, he remained where he was and faced the soldiers unafraid.

The captain certainly didn't use the title "man of God" as a compliment to Elijah or as a confession of his own faith, for "man of God" was a common synonym for "prophet." Elijah's reply meant, "Since you called me a man of God, let me prove it to you. My God will deal with you according to your own words." The fire that came from heaven killed all fifty-one men. This judgment was repeated when the second company of fifty arrived. Note that the second captain ordered Elijah to "come down quickly." Don't keep your king waiting! The memory of the contest on Mount Carmel should have warned the king and his soldiers that Elijah could bring fire from heaven (1 Kings 18).

We must not interpret these two displays of God's wrath as evidence of irritation on the part of Elijah or injustice on the part of God. After all, weren't the soldiers only doing their duty and obeying their commander? These two episodes of fiery judgment were dramatic messages from the Lord that the king and the nation had better repent or they would all taste the judgment of God. The people had forgotten the lessons of Mount Carmel, and these two judgments reminded them that the God of Israel was "a consuming fire" (Deut. 4:24 and 9:3; Heb. 12:29). King Ahaziah was a proud man who sacrificed two captains and one hundred men in a futile attempt to prevent his own death. These were not innocent men, the victims of their ruler's whims, but guilty men who were willing to do what the king commanded. Had they adopted the attitude of the third captain, they too would have lived.[2]

Disobedience (vv. 13-18). Insisting that Elijah obey him, the king sent a third company of soldiers, but this time the captain showed wisdom and humility. Unlike the king and the two previous captains, he submitted himself to the Lord and His servant. The third captain's plea for himself and his men was evidence that he acknowledged Elijah's authority and that he would do God's servant no harm. The Lord's words in verse 15 suggest that the danger lay in the hands of the captains and not in the hands of the king. Perhaps the king had ordered them to kill Elijah en route to the palace or after he had left the palace. If the king had to die, he would at least take Elijah with him!

The king was in bed when Elijah confronted him and for the second time told him he would die. How many times must the

Lord repeat His message to a wicked sinner? The king would leave this world with "you will surely die" ringing in his ears, yet he refused to obey the Word of God. Again, we're reminded of Herod's response to John the Baptist, for Herod listened to John's words but still wouldn't repent (Mark 6:20). After about two years on the throne, Ahaziah did die, just as Elijah had predicted, and his younger brother Jehoram (or Joram) became king. Note that the current king of Judah was also named Jehoram (v. 17). To avoid confusion, we shall refer to Ahaziah's brother, the king of Israel, as Joram, and Jehoshaphat's son, the king of Judah, as Jehoram.

Before leaving this passage, we need to remind ourselves that a proud and unrepentant world will one day experience the fire of the wrath of God. It will happen "when the Lord Jesus is revealed from heaven with His mighty angels, in flaming fire taking vengeance on those who do not know God, and on those who do not obey the gospel of our Lord Jesus Christ. These shall be punished with everlasting destruction from the presence of the Lord and from the glory of His power" (2 Thes. 1:7-9, NKJV). God "commands all men everywhere to repent" (Acts 17:30, NKJV), which means that those who do not repent are rebels against the Lord. The gospel isn't only a message to believe; it's also a mandate to obey.

God wants us to remember (2 Kings 2:1-6)
King Ahaziah died but Elijah didn't die! He was taken up into heaven in a whirlwind, accompanied by fiery horses drawing a chariot of fire. Like Enoch of old, he walked with God and then suddenly went to be with God (Gen. 5:21-24; Heb. 11:5). Both men illustrate the catching away of the saints when Jesus returns (1 Thes. 4:13-18). But before Elijah left Elisha to carry on the work, he walked with his successor from Gilgal to beyond the Jordan, and what a walk that must have been! The Lord had at least three purposes in mind when He led these two servants to walk together.

Taking advantage of the present. Elisha knew that his master was going to leave him (vv. 1, 3, 5), and he wanted to be with him to

11

the very end, listen to his counsel and learn from him. It appears that Elijah wanted Elisha to tarry behind and let him go on alone, but this was merely a test of Elisha's devotion. When Elijah threw his mantle on Elisha and made him his successor, the younger man promised, "I will follow you" (1 Kings 19:20), and he kept that promise.

During the years that the two men had worked together, surely they came to love and appreciate one another in a deeper way. "It is not good that the man should be alone" (Gen. 2:18) applies to ministry as well as marriage. Moses and Aaron labored together, and David and Jonathan encouraged each other. Paul journeyed first with Barnabas and then with Silas, and Dr. Luke seemed to be a regular companion to the apostle. Even our Lord sent out His disciples two-by-two (Mark 6:7; see Ecc. 4:9-12). We are not only fellow workers with the Lord, but also with the Lord's people, and there must be no competition as we serve the same Lord together (John 4:34-38; 1 Cor. 3:1-9).

We never know when a friend and fellow worker will be taken from us. God told Elisha that Elijah was leaving him, but we don't know when it is our time or a friend's time to go to heaven. What great opportunities we miss by wasting time on trifles when we could be learning from each other about the Lord and His Word! It rejoices my heart when I see younger Christians and Christian workers appreciating the "senior saints," the veterans of Christian service, and learning from them. One day, these "giants" will be called home and we'll no longer be able to learn from them.

These two men represented different generations and opposite personalities, yet they were able to walk together. What a rebuke this is to those in the church who label the generations and separate them from each other. I heard one youthful pastor say that he didn't want anybody in his church over the age of forty, and I wondered where he would get the wise counsel that usually comes with maturity. I thank God for the "Elijahs" in my life who were patient with me and took time to instruct me. Now I'm trying to share that same blessing with others.

Preparing for the future. At Bethel, Jericho, and Gilgal, the two men visited the "sons of the prophets" (vv. 5, 7, 15; 4:1, 38-40; 6:1, 7; 9:1; see 1 Kings 20:35), companies of dedicated men who were called of God to study the Scriptures and teach the people. Samuel led one of these "schools" at Ramah (1 Sam. 7:17; 28:3; see 10:5, 10; 19:20-23). These groups would be similar to the mentoring groups in our churches, or even like our Bible schools and colleges. The work of the Lord is always one generation short of extinction and we must be faithful to obey 2 Timothy 2:2— "And the things that you have heard from me among many witnesses, commit these to faithful men who will be able to teach others also" (NKJV).

These young prophets knew that their master was about to leave them, so these final meetings must have been very emotional. We have "farewell messages" in Scripture from Moses (the Book of Deuteronomy), Joshua (Josh. 23–24), David (1 Chron. 28–29), Jesus (John 13–16), and Paul (Acts 20:17-38 and 2 Tim.), but the Lord didn't record for us what Elijah said to his beloved students. Certainly he told them to obey Elisha just as they had obeyed him, to remain true to the Word of God and to do everything God told them to do as they battled against idolatry in the land. It was their responsibility to call the people back to obeying God's covenant (Deut. 27–30) so that He might be pleased to bless and heal their land.

During the years that I was privileged to instruct seminary students, I occasionally heard some of them say, "Why should we attend school? Charles Spurgeon never went to seminary, and neither did Campbell Morgan or D. L. Moody!" I would usually reply, "If any of you are Spurgeons, Morgans, or Moodys, we'll no doubt discover it and give you permission to stop your education. But let me remind you that both Spurgeon and Moody founded schools for training preachers, and Campbell Morgan was once president of a training college and also taught at a number of schools. Meanwhile, back to our studies."

God has different ways of training His servants, but He still expects the older generation to pass along to the younger generation the treasures of truth that were given to them by those who went before, "the faith . . . once for all delivered to the saints" (Jude 3, NKJV).

Reviewing the past. Gilgal, Bethel, Jericho, and the Jordan River were important places in Hebrew history, each of them carrying a significant message. Before he left the land and went to heaven, Elijah wanted to visit these sites one last time and take Elisha with him. Our eternal God doesn't reside in special places, but we who are creatures of time and history need these visible reminders to help us remember and better understand what God has done for His people. The past is not an anchor to hold us back but a rudder to guide us, and the Lord can use these "tangible memories" to strengthen our faith. The British poet W. H. Auden wrote, "Man is a history-making creature who can neither repeat his past nor leave it behind." It's important for us to remember what God did in the past and to pass this treasure along to our children and grandchildren (Pss. 48:9-14; 71:17-18; 78:1-8; 145:4). That's one of the major themes of Moses' farewell address to the new generation about to enter the Promised Land (Deut. 4:9-10; 6:4-9; 11:19-21; 29:29). "Remember" is found fourteen times in Deuteronomy and "forget" at least nine times.

Gilgal (v. 1) was the first place the Israelites camped after they crossed the Jordan River and entered the Promised Land (Josh. 4:19-20). It was there that the new generation of Jewish men submitted to circumcision and officially became "sons of the covenant" (Josh. 5:2-9). Gilgal was the place of new beginnings and Elijah wanted his successor to remember that. Each new generation is an opportunity for God to raise up new leaders, and each time His people repent and return to Him, He can restore them and renew them. At that time, Gilgal was the center of idolatrous worship (Hos. 4:15; 9:15; 12:11; Amos 4:4 and 5:5), but Elijah didn't abandon it.

From Gilgal the two men walked to Bethel (vv. 2-3), about fifteen miles west of Gilgal. Abraham worshiped there (Gen. 12:8; 13:3) and so did Jacob. It was at Bethel that Jacob saw the angels ascending and descending the ladder (or staircase) that reached to heaven. There he heard God promise to be with him and care for him (Gen. 28:11-19). Bethel means "house of God," and there Jacob worshiped the Lord and vowed to obey Him. Years later, Jacob returned to Bethel and, like Abraham (Gen. 13:3), made a new beginning in his walk with the Lord (Gen. 35). King Jeroboam had put a golden calf at Bethel and made it the site of idolatrous worship (1 Kings 12:26-32; Amos 3:14; 4:4-6), but Elijah looked beyond the city's present desecration to the time when it was a place of blessing and renewal.

At Bethel, the students spoke to Elisha about his master's departure. Perhaps they thought they knew something that nobody else knew, an attitude not uncommon among some students. The same scene was repeated when Elijah and Elisha arrived at Jericho (v. 5). In both cities, Elisha politely assured the students that he was aware of what was about to happen, but that their discussing it only added to the pain of his separation from his master. Their approach to what God was doing was purely cerebral, but to Elisha, the loss of his beloved master brought pain to his heart. The mark of a true student of the Scriptures is a burning heart, not a big head (Luke 24:32; 1 Cor. 8:1).

The two men then went fifteen miles west to Jericho, the site of Joshua's first victory in the Promised Land (Josh. 5:13–6:27). It was also the place where Achan disobeyed and took of the spoils that belonged to the Lord alone, a sin that led to Israel's defeat at Ai (Josh. 7). Certainly the wonderful victory at Jericho showed Israel how to conquer the land: get your orders from the Lord; obey them by faith, no matter how foolish they may seem; give all the glory to Him alone. The two times Joshua failed to follow this formula, he experienced defeat (Josh. 7, 9). Joshua had put under a curse anybody who rebuilt Jericho (Josh. 6:26), but during the reign of evil King Ahab, the city was rebuilt (1 Kings 16:34). Jericho would remind Elisha of the victory of faith, the tragedy of sin and the majesty of the Lord who deserves all the glory.

Elijah and Elisha walked five miles east and came to the Jordan River, and surely the record in Joshua 1–4 came into their minds and into their conversation. The Lord opened the Red Sea to let His people out of Egypt (Ex. 12–15), and then He opened the Jordan River to let them into their inheritance. What good is freedom if you don't claim your inheritance? As the nation followed the ark of the covenant, the Lord opened the swollen waters of the river, and the people passed over on dry land! To commemorate this miracle, Joshua built a monument in the midst of the river and another one on the shore. Nothing is too hard for the Lord, for with God, all things are possible! *And Elijah duplicated that great miracle!*

This is a good place to point out the similarities between Moses and Elijah. Both opened bodies of water, Moses the Red Sea (Ex. 14:16, 21, 26) and Elijah the Jordan River. Both called down fire from heaven (Ex. 9:24; Lev. 9:24; Num. 11:1 and 16:35), Both men saw the Lord provide food, Moses the manna (Ex. 16) and quails (Num. 11), and Elijah the oil and flour for the widow, plus his own meals (1 Kings 17:1-16). In the land of Egypt, Moses prayed and God altered the weather, and Elijah prayed and God stopped the rain and then three years later started the rain again. Moses gave the law to the people of Israel and Elijah called them to repent and return to the true and living God. Both were associated with mountains (Sinai and Carmel), and both made journeys through the wilderness. Both men had unique endings to their lives: God buried Moses in a grave nobody can find, and God carried Elijah to heaven by a whirlwind. Both Moses and Elijah were privileged to be present with Jesus on the Mount of Transfiguration (Matt. 17:4; Mark 9:5; Luke 9:33).

Elijah is a good model for believers to imitate when it comes to the inevitability of one day leaving this earth, either through death or the rapture of the church. He didn't sit around and do nothing, but instead visited three of the prophetic schools and no doubt ministered to the students. He didn't say to his successor "I'm going to leave you" and thus dwell on the negative, but said "I'm going to Bethel—to Jericho—to the Jordan" and kept busy until the very moment the Lord called him. Even more, he didn't ask his successor to give him anything, because we can't take anything in our hands from earth to heaven (1 Tim. 6:7), but instead he offered to give Elisha a gift before the end came.[3] One of the best gifts we can leave is a prepared servant of God to take our place!

God rewards service (2 Kings 2:7-12)
As Elijah and Elisha stood by the Jordan River, they were watched by fifty of the sons of the prophets, men who stood afar off. They knew that Elijah was going to leave that day (vv. 3 and 5), but they didn't know how he would depart or when God would call him. It's likely that only Elisha actually saw Elisha go up into heaven (v. 10), and after the prophet disappeared, the fifty students thought he hadn't really left them (vv. 16-18). They saw Elijah open the waters of the Jordan and close them again, and they saw Elisha repeat the miracle, but they didn't see what Elisha saw when the whirlwind took Elijah to heaven. The fifty men were spectators that saw only part of what happened, but Elisha was a participant in the miracle and the heir to Elijah's ministry.

Elijah didn't give his successor three wishes; he simply asked him to name the one gift he wanted more than anything else. Every leader needs to be right in his priorities, and Elisha had a ready answer: he wanted a double portion of the spirit of his master. This was not a request for twice as much of the Holy Spirit, or for a ministry twice as great as that of Elijah, but for a greater degree of the inner spirit that motivated the great prophet. The request was based on Deuteronomy 21:17, the law of inheritance for the firstborn. Though there were many "sons of the prophets," Elisha saw himself as Elijah's "firstborn son" who deserved the double inheritance that Moses commanded. Like a firstborn son serving a father, Elisha had walked with Elijah and attended to his needs (3:11; 1 Kings 19:21), but the only inheritance he desired was a double measure of his master's inner spirit of courage, faithfulness, faith in God, and obedience to God's will. In saying this, Elisha was accepting the prophetic ministry that Elijah had begun and declaring that he would carry it on to completion, with God's help.

Elijah was honest with his friend and told him that such a gift was not his to grant, for only the Lord could do it. However, if the Lord allowed Elisha to see his translation from earth to heaven, that would be proof that his request had been granted. Then it happened! As the two friends walked along talking, a fiery chariot drawn by fiery horses came between them, and a whirlwind lifted Elijah out of sight—*and Elisha saw it happen!* This meant his request had been granted and the Lord had equipped him to continue the ministry of Elijah. Elijah was certainly the "prophet of fire," for Scripture records at least three instances of his bringing fire from heaven (1 Kings 18:38; 2 Kings 1:10 and 12), so it was right that God send fiery horses and a chariot of fire to accompany His servant to glory.

Elisha's response was one of grief, like a son mourning over the loss of a beloved father. But he paid great tribute to Elijah when he called him "the chariot of Israel and its horseman" (v. 12). This one man was the equivalent of a whole army! In His covenant with Israel, the Lord promised that, if the nation obeyed Him, He would enable a hundred Israelites to chase ten thousand enemy soldiers (Lev. 26:6-8), and Moses promised that God would cause one man to chase a thousand and two men to chase ten thousand (Deut. 32:30). One with God is a majority.

God honors faith (2 Kings 2:13-25)
Elijah was gone and Elisha couldn't turn to him for help, but the God of Israel was still on the throne. From now on, Elisha's faith would put him in touch with the power of God and enable him to accomplish God's work in Israel. Three miracles are recorded here, each with spiritual messages that we need to understand today.

Crossing the river (vv.13-18). Why did Elijah leave the Promised Land and go to the other side of the Jordan? Was he abandoning his own country and people? Certainly God's whirlwind could have lifted him just as easily from Bethel or Jericho. Technically, Elijah was still in Israelite territory when he crossed the river, since Reuben and Gad and the half tribe of Manasseh had their inheritance east of the Jordan. But there was more involved. By taking Elisha west of the Jordan, Elijah forced him to trust God to get him across the river and back into the land! Elijah's successor was now like Joshua: he had to believe that God could and would open the river for him. The students who were watching must have wondered what their new leader would do.

In taking up Elijah's mantle, Elisha was making it clear that he accepted the responsibilities involved as he succeeded the great prophet and continued his work. By using the mantle to open the waters of the Jordan, he was declaring that his faith was not in the departed prophet but in the ever-present living God. Certainly we ought to honor the memories and accomplishments of departed leaders. "Remember those who led you, who spoke the word of God to you; and considering the result of their conduct, imitate their faith" (Heb. 13:7, NASB). But too many dead founders and leaders still control their former ministries from their graves, and their successors find it difficult to make the changes needed for survival. Elisha didn't make that mistake, for he called on the God of Elijah to assist him, and the Lord honored his faith. Elisha wasn't a clone of Elijah, but the two men had this in common: they both had faith in the true and living God. That's why Hebrews 13:7 commands us to remember past spiritual leaders and "imitate their faith."

Elisha's miraculous crossing of the Jordan River not only demonstrated the power of God and the faith of His servant, but it also announced to the sons of the prophets that Elisha was their new leader. When God opened the Jordan so Israel could cross, He used that miracle to magnify Joshua's name and declare that His hand was upon the new leader (Josh. 3:7-8; 4:14). A. W. Tozer used to say that "it takes more than a ballot to make a leader," and he was right. Regardless of how they were trained or chosen, true spiritual leaders assure their followers of their divine calling by demonstrating the power of God in their lives. "Therefore by their fruits you will know them" (Matt. 7:20, NKJV).

The fifty sons of the prophets who saw Elisha cross the river on dry ground had no problem submitting to him and accepting his leadership because God's power was evident in his ministry.

But the fifty students didn't believe that their former leader had actually gone to heaven; they asked for on-site verification. God had openly demonstrated that Elisha was their new leader, so why search for Elijah? And why would the Lord catch His servant up in the whirlwind only to abandon him in some forsaken part of the country? Is that the kind of God they served? Furthermore, it was impossible for the students to search out every part of the land, so why even begin? The entire enterprise was ridiculous and Elisha permitted the search only because he was annoyed by their repeated requests. New leaders must not be vexed by the interest their followers have in their former leader. When the search parties returned to Elisha at Jericho, he at least had the privilege of telling them, "I told you so!"

Healing the bad water (vv. 19-22). Not only did Elisha enjoy the loyalty of the sons of the prophets, but the leaders of Jericho also respected him and sought his help. It should be no surprise to us that the water at Jericho was distasteful and the soil unproductive, for the city was under a curse (Josh. 6:26). The Old Testament Jew thought of salt in terms of God's covenant (Num. 18:19) and personal purity in worship (Lev. 2:13). The phrase "to eat salt" meant "to share hospitality," so that salt implied friendship and loyalty between people and between God and man. The salt didn't purify the water or heal the soil; that was the work of God. This miracle reminds us of the miracle at Marah ("bitter"), when Moses threw in a piece of wood and healed the water (Ex. 15:22-26). At Marah, God revealed Himself to His people as "Jehovah-Rapha—the Lord who heals."

If you visit Jericho today, tour guides will point out "Elisha's fountain" and invite you to take a drink.

Once more, we have a miracle that speaks of a new beginning. Elisha even emptied the salt from a new bowl. The miracle was an "action sermon" that reminded the people that the blessings of God were for a nation that was loyal to His covenant. To disobey His law meant to forfeit His blessings (Deut. 28:15ff).

Judging the mockers (vv. 23-25). This event took place at Bethel, one of the centers for idol worship in the land (1 Kings

12:28-33; Amos 7:13). The Hebrew word translated "little children" in the KJV really means "youths" or "young men." It refers to people from twelve to thirty years old who were able to discern right from wrong and make their own decisions. This was not a group of playful children making a clever joke but a gang of smart-aleck youths maliciously ridiculing God and God's servant.

"Go up" refers to the recent ascension of Elijah to heaven. Fifty men saw Elijah vanish from the earth in an instant, and certainly they reported what had happened and the event was discussed widely. The youths were saying, "If you are a man of God, why don't you get out of here and go to heaven the way Elijah did? We're glad he's gone and we wish you would follow him!" For a young person to call any grown man "bald head" would be a gross affront, and to repeat the nickname would make the offense even worse. Gray hair was a "crown of glory" (Prov. 16:31) among the Jews, but baldness was a rare thing among them and by some people was considered a disgrace (Isa. 3:24).

What we have here is a gang of irreverent and disrespectful ruffians mocking God's servant and repeating words they probably heard at home or in the marketplace. Because he knew the Word of God, Elisha understood that what they were doing was a violation of God's covenant, so he called down a curse upon them. (One of the covenant warnings was that God would send wild beasts to attack the people. See Lev. 26:21-22.) These young men were not showing respect to the Lord God of Israel, to Elijah or to Elisha, so they had to be judged. The two bears mauled the youths but didn't kill them, and for the rest of their days, their scars reminded everybody that they couldn't trifle with the Lord and get away with it.

You frequently find the Lord sending special judgments at the beginning of a new period in Bible history, as though God were issuing a warning to His people that the new beginning doesn't means that the old rules have been changed. After the tabernacle ministry began, God killed Nadab and Abihu for offering "strange fire" before the Lord (Lev. 10). After Israel's first victory in the Promised Land, God ordered Achan to be slain because he took treasures from the spoils of war that were wholly dedicated to God (Josh. 7). At the outset of David's reign in Jerusalem, he had the ark of the covenant brought to the city, and Uzzah was killed for touching it (2 Sam. 6:1-7). When Ananias and Sapphira lied to the leaders in the early church, God took their lives (Acts 5). Now, at the beginning of Elisha's ministry, the mauling of the youths gave fair warning that the Lord God of Elijah was still reigning and still took His covenant seriously.

The attitude displayed by these youths, as it spread through the land, is what eventually led to the fall of both Samaria and Judah. "And the Lord God of their fathers sent warnings to them by His messengers. . . . But they mocked the messengers of God, despised His words, and scoffed at His prophets, until the wrath of the Lord arose against His people, till there was no remedy" (2 Chron. 36:15-16, NKJV).

Elisha had been with Elijah at Gilgal, Bethel and Jericho, and had crossed the Jordan with him, but now he went to Mount Carmel, the scene of Elijah's greatest triumph. As far as we know, Elisha wasn't there when Elijah called down fire from heaven. Perhaps as Elisha visited the place where the altar had stood, he meditated on what the Lord had done and he was renewed in his spirit. No doubt he gave thanks to God that he was part of such a wonderful heritage. But you can't live in the past, so he left that sacred place and headed for Samaria, capital city of the Northern Kingdom and home of King Joram, son of Ahab. There he would be involved in a war involving Israel, Judah, and Moab against Edom, and Elisha would provide the weapon that would win the battle for the three kings.

TWO

Amazing Grace!

From the outset of his ministry, Elisha proved himself to be a worker of miracles like his master and predecessor Elijah, for he opened the Jordan River and crossed on dry land, and then he purified the water at Jericho. Except for calling down judgment on a group of arrogant young men (2:23-25), Elisha's miracles were primarily revelations of God's grace and mercy. Elijah reminds us of John the Baptist with his ax, winnowing fork, and baptism of fire (Matt. 3:1-12; Luke 1:17); but Elisha reminds us of our Savior who had compassion on the multitudes and "went about doing good" (Acts 10:38). The six miracles recorded in these two chapters certainly magnify the grace of God.

Grace defeats the enemy (2 Kings 3:1-27)
When Ahaziah died, his brother Joram became king of Israel (1:17). He was also called Jehoram, but since that was also the name of Jehoshaphat's son and the coregent of Judah, we'll distinguish the two rulers by calling the king of Israel Joram. Being a son of Ahab and Jezebel, the new king was hardly a godly man, but at least he removed an image dedicated to Baal (1 Kings 16:32-33) and he showed some respect for Elisha. However, nei-

23

ther Baal worship nor the golden calves were removed from the land during his reign, and the image of Baal that Joram removed found its way back and Jehu had to destroy it (10:27).

A costly rebellion (vv. 4-8; see 1:1). The land of Moab was especially suited for raising sheep, but an annual tribute to Israel of 100,000 lambs and the wool of 100,000 rams was certainly demanding. Ahab's death and Ahaziah's brief reign of less than two years gave Mesha opportunity to rebel. When Joram, a younger man, took the throne of Israel, it seemed like an opportune time for Moab to break the yoke once and for all. But Joram didn't want to lose all that free income, nor did he want his people to think he was a weak ruler, so he took a military census and prepared for war.

Jehoram, now co-regent of Judah, was married to Joram's sister Athaliah, so it seemed only right for Joram to ask King Jehoshaphat to go with him to punish Moab. A year before, the Moabites and Ammonites had declared war on Judah and Jehoshaphat, had soundly defeated them with the Lord's help (2 Chron. 20). Joram wanted allies like that at his side! They two kings decided not to attack from the north because the northern border of Moab was heavily fortified and the Ammonites might interfere, but to make an attack from around the southern extremity of the Dead Sea. Joram's army would march south through Judah and pick up Jehoshaphat's men, and then both armies would march through Edom and join with the Edomite army at the more vulnerable southern border of Moab.

A needy army (vv. 9-14). The plan was a good one. Joram's army left Samaria and after a three-day march joined Jehoshaphat's army in Judah, probably at Jerusalem. Then both armies proceeded south to Edom, a journey of about four days. So, after this seven-day march, the armies arrived at the valley at the southern end of the Dead Sea, between the mountains of Judah and Moab. Everything was going well except that they were out of water. The soldiers were thirsty and so were the baggage animals and the cattle brought along for food.

Conveniently forgetting that his father's god Baal was the rain god, King Joram responded to the situation by blaming the Lord for their plight (v. 10). Jehoshaphat, on the other hand, suggested that they consult the Lord and see what He wanted them to do. He had given the same advice to Ahab years before when they had joined forces to fight the Syrians (1 Kings 22). Joram didn't know any prophets of the Lord and didn't even know that Elisha was in the area. One of his own officers had to tell him that the prophet had joined the troops, certainly by the leading of the Lord. At that hour, Elisha was the most valuable man in the combined armies of the three nations. Elisha had compared Elijah to the army of Israel (2:12), but now Elisha was more powerful than three armies!

We aren't told where Elisha was, but the three kings humbled themselves and went there to ask for his help. When Jehoshaphat joined with Ahab to fight the Syrians, the Lord's prophet rebuked him for compromising (2 Chron. 19:1-4); but now, the presence of a descendant of King David was the key to victory. Elisha made it clear that he wasn't helping Joram, son of Ahab, but Jehoshaphat, son of David. Once again, it is God's covenant with David that introduces the grace of God and brings about God's rescue of His people. Joram's reply still smacked of unbelief: "We're all in this together and are in danger of being defeated!" But when it came to confronting kings, Elisha was as fearless as his mentor Elijah.

A *divine intervention* (*vv. 15-27*). The music of the harpist brought quietness to the prophet's mind and heart and helped to facilitate his communion with the Lord. Then Elisha revealed God's plan. The kings were to command their soldiers to dig ditches or pits in the dry valley. God would send rain in the distant mountains, but the Moabite army wouldn't know it because there would be no sound of wind or storm. The rain would create a flood that would move down from the mountains and cover the arid plain. Some of the water would collect in the pits or trenches and be available for the men and beasts to drink. But God would also use those pools to deceive and defeat the Moabite army. Elisha didn't explain how.

Then Elisha added that God would enable the three armies to defeat the Moabites, but it must be a complete victory. They were to tear down, stone by stone, all the fortified cities in Moab and throw the stones in the fields. They must also cut down the trees and stop up the wells.[1] In other words, the three armies should so destroy Moab's resources that they would not be able to regroup and start fighting back.

The priests back in Jerusalem were offering the early morning sacrifice when the rain that fell in the mountains came flooding into the valley. It filled the trenches and formed pools on the earth, and the soldiers, cattle, and baggage animals were all able to drink to the full. *But the Moabite army assembled at the border knew nothing about the rain!* God arranged that the reflection of the sun on the pools gave the illusion of blood, and the Moabites were deceived into thinking that the three armies had slaughtered each other. (This had happened to the armies of Moab, Ammon and Edom when they attacked King Jehoshaphat, 2 Chron. 20:22-30.) Confident of their safety and the opportunity for wealth, the Moabites attacked the camp of the three kings and were soundly defeated and chased away.

The three armies obeyed God's command and moved into Moab bent on destroying their cities and doing as much damage to their natural resources as possible. The king of Moab and his army retreated to Kir Haraseth, the capital at that time, and the invading armies laid siege to it but couldn't break through. The king of Moab tried to get through the lines to Edom, perhaps to persuade his former allies to help him, but the plan didn't work. His final step was to turn to his god Chemosh and offer him the life of the crown prince. He did this publicly, on the wall of the city, and the result was that the armies called off the siege and returned to their own lands.

A strange ending (v. 27) Joram succeeded in punishing Moab for breaking their agreement, but what was it that ended the war? The phrase "great indignation against Israel" (KJV and NKJV) has been translated "the fury against Israel" (NIV), "there came great wrath against Israel" (NASB), "the anger against Israel was great"

(NLT), and "Great indignation came upon Israel" (*Berkeley*). The *New English Bible* reads, "The Israelites were filled with such consternation at this sight, that they struck camp and returned to their own land." The marginal reading is, "There was such great anger against the Israelites."

We can't believe that the false god Chemosh did anything to stop the invaders or that Jehovah would allow a brutal pagan sacrifice to take glory from His name. "I am the Lord: that is my name: and my glory will I not give to another, neither my praise to graven images" (Isa. 42:8). This leaves us with three possibilities. Perhaps the sacrifice gave fresh courage and zeal to the Moabites so that their army attacked with new enthusiasm and drove the invaders back. Or, perhaps the Israelites were so disgusted at the sacrifice that they packed up and left, and the other two kings followed with their armies. Human sacrifices were forbidden by the Mosaic Law (Lev. 20:1-5) and Jehoshaphat may have felt guilty that his siege had caused the death of the crown prince. But the three armies had slain many people as they moved through Moab, and it's not likely that they regretted the death of the king's successor. Furthermore, the emphasis is on Israel and not Judah, and King Joram of Israel wouldn't be upset at the offering of a human sacrifice. He came from a family of murderers!

If the Lord sent His wrath against Israel, why did He do so? Did He judge King Joram and his army alone (Israel = the Northern Kingdom) or Israel and Judah together? Throughout the text, "Israel" refers to the Northern Kingdom and not the united tribes, so Joram and the army of Israel must have been the target. Twice Joram had questioned whether Jehovah could or would do anything (vv. 10, 13), and Elisha made it clear that he wasn't paying any attention to the apostate king (vv. 13-14). Yet Joram was sharing in a great victory because of the faith of the king of Judah! Perhaps the Lord demonstrated His wrath against the army of Israel alone to teach Joram a lesson, just as He sent drought and fire from heaven to teach his father Ahab a lesson. When Israel had to leave the field, the other two kings left with them, and this ended the siege. The capital city was not destroyed and the Moabite king and his forces were neither captured nor killed, so it was an incomplete victory. However, for the sake of the house of David, God in His grace gave victory to the three kings.

Grace pays the debt (2 Kings 4:1-7)[2]
From the great international conflict, Elisha returned to the concerns of the schools of the prophets, for a true spiritual leader has a concern for individuals. He followed the example of his mentor Elijah who had ministered to families (1 Kings 17:8-24). The fact that the woman was a widow and the mother of two sons shows that the sons of the prophets weren't a celibate monastic group. Elisha knew this particular man and that he had a reputation for godliness. His death would have ended whatever income he earned, and for a widow to raise two sons unaided would have been a difficult thing at that time. Even dedicated people training for ministry have their trials and difficulties.

According to Hebrew law, a creditor could take the debtor and his children as servants, but he was not to treat them like slaves (Ex. 21:1-11; Lev. 25:29-31; Deut. 15:1-11). It would be heartbreaking for this woman to lose her husband to death and her two sons to servitude, but God is the "judge of the widows" (Deut. 10:18; Pss. 68:5; 146:9) and He sent Elisha to help her.[3]

God often begins with what we already have. Moses had a rod in his hand, and God used that to accomplish great things (Ex. 4:2). Peter and his partners had fishing nets in their hands (Luke 5), and the lad had a few loaves and fishes (John 6). All that the poor widow had was a little oil in a vessel, but "little is much when God is in it." Most of her neighbors would have unused empty vessels sitting around, so she wasn't robbing anybody by borrowing them, and once she had sold the oil, she could return the vessels. Elisha instructed her to shut the door so that nobody would see that a miracle was occurring in her house, and no doubt she warned her sons to keep quiet. The amount of oil she received was limited by the number of vessels she had, and that was controlled by her faith. (See also 13:10-19.) "According to your faith let it be to you" (Matt. 9:29, NKJV). When she sold the oil, she had enough money to pay off the debt and maintain herself and her two sons.

The Lord doesn't always perform miracles of this kind to help us pay our debts, but He does meet our needs if we trust and obey. If we give everything to Him, He can make a little go a long way. This miracle also reminds us of the greatest miracle of all, the gracious forgiveness of our debts to the Lord through faith in Jesus Christ (Luke 7:36-50; Eph. 1:7; Col. 2:13). It didn't cost Elisha anything for God to provide the needed money to pay the debt, but it cost Jesus Christ His life to be able forgive us our sins.

Grace imparts the life (2 Kings 4:8-37)
Shunem was about twenty miles northwest of Abel-meholah, Elisha's hometown, and twenty-five miles or so beyond Shunem was Mount Carmel (see v. 25). The average traveler on foot could cover fifteen to twenty miles per day, so Shunem was the perfect half-way point for Elisha whenever he went to Mount Carmel to pray, meditate, and seek the Lord in a new way. Since Mount Carmel was a very special place because of Elijah's ministry, perhaps there was also a school of the prophets there.

A great woman (vv. 8-10). The unnamed woman was great in social standing and in wealth. But she was also great in perception, for she noticed that Elijah often passed that way on his ministry trips. She also discerned that he was a man of God, and she wanted to serve the Lord by serving His prophet. We get the impression that her husband lacked his wife's spiritual insight, but at least he didn't oppose her hospitality to the itinerant preacher. He permitted her to have a permanent "prophet's chamber" built on the roof of the house and to outfit it with a lamp, a table and chair,[4] and a bed. It was large enough to walk around in (v. 35) and apparently offered room enough for Gehazi, Elisha's servant (v. 13). The woman also saw to it that the two men were fed.

In this day of motels and hotels, hospitality to God's people, and especially God's servants, is becoming a neglected ministry and a lost blessing. Yet, one of the qualifications for an elder is "given to hospitality" (1 Tim. 3:2; Titus 1:8), and Hebrews 13:2 exhorts all believers to practice this virtue (see Gen. 18). We should open our hearts and homes to others and not complain about it (1 Peter 4:9).

A great gift (vv. 11-17). The prophet and his servant were resting in the room when Elisha expressed a desire to do something special for the woman because of her kindness to them, and he asked Gehazi to call her so he could discuss the matter with her. Elisha addressed his words to Gehazi, possibly because the woman held Elisha in such high regard that she didn't feel worthy to speak with him. But her reply was humble and brief: "I am content among my own people." She didn't want Elisha to intercede with the great because she had no desire to be treated like a great person. She ministered to them because she wanted to serve the Lord.

After she left the prophet's chamber, Gehazi suggested that she might want a son. Her husband was older than she, so perhaps conception was impossible; but if God could do it for Abraham and Sarah, He could do it for them. It was likely that her husband would precede her in death, and without a family, she would be left alone. Gehazi called her a second time, and this time Elijah spoke to her personally. He gave her a promise that sounded very much like God's words to Abraham and Sarah (v. 16; Gen. 17:21; 18:14). How many blessings husbands with nominal faith have received because of the dedication of their godly wives! The promise was fulfilled and the woman gave birth to a son. Grace brought life where once there had been no life.

A great sorrow (vv. 18-28). The boy was still a child when these events occurred, for his mother was able to hold him on her lap and carry his limp body up to Elijah's chamber on the roof (vv. 20-21). The cause of the lad's illness isn't specified, but perhaps the heat of the harvest season affected him. The mother called to the father in the field and asked him to provide her with a servant and a donkey, but she didn't inform him that the boy had died. The fact that she was leaving suggested that the boy was safe, probably taking a nap. No doubt she feared her husband would order instant burial, for nobody wants a corpse in the house during the hot harvest season. Her husband wondered why she wanted to see Elisha when it wasn't a special holy day, but her only reply was, "Peace—*shalom*." She would also say this to Gehazi (v. 26).

Gehazi's attitude toward the woman's coming reveals a dark streak in his character that shows up even more in the next chapter (v. 27; see Matt. 15:23; 19:13-15). Perhaps the woman and her servant intruded on their afternoon siesta. But Elisha discerned that something was wrong that the Lord hadn't revealed to him. Even Jesus occasionally asked for information (Mark 5:9; 9:21; John 11:34). Of course the woman was bitter and heartbroken, and it sounds like she was blaming Elisha for the tragedy. She hadn't asked for a son, and if Elisha and Gehazi hadn't interfered, her joy wouldn't have been snatched from her.

A great miracle (vv. 29-37). The woman and the servant must have ridden very fast to get to Mount Carmel in time for Elisha and Gehazi to return home with her the same day; and the animal must have been exhausted from such a strenuous trip in the harvest sun. Why did Elisha send Gehazi ahead? He was probably the younger of the two men and could run faster and get to the house much quicker. It was important that somebody get back to guard the corpse so that the father wouldn't discover it and have it buried. Gehazi laid his staff on the boy's body, but nothing happened. (Was this because of what was hidden in his heart?) The woman rode the donkey and Elisha followed after her, but we aren't told that he received special power as Elijah did when he ran before Ahab's chariot (1 Kings 18:46).

Once again the door was shut on a miracle (4:4; and see Luke 8:51). First, the prophet prayed, and then, following the example of Elijah (1 Kings 17:17-24), he stretched himself out over the corpse. He got up and walked in the room, no doubt praying and seeking God's power, and then he lay on the boy a second time. This time the boy came back to life, sneezed seven times and opened his eyes. The text doesn't explain the significance of the sneezes, unless it was God's way of expelling something toxic from his lungs. You would think that Elisha would have been overjoyed to take the boy downstairs to his mother, but instead, he called Gehazi who in turn called the mother.[5] See Hebrews 11:35.

But the story doesn't end there (see 8:1-6). Later, when Elisha announced the coming of a seven-year famine, he also advised the woman to relocate, so she went to dwell with the Philistines. When she returned to claim her property, Gehazi was speaking with the king and telling him about the resurrection of the boy, and his mother showed up in the palace! The king authorized the officials to return her property to her along with whatever income she had lost because of her absence. The death of the boy turned out to be a blessing in disguise.

Only God's grace can impart life, whether to a dead womb or to a dead boy, and only God's grace can impart spiritual life to the dead sinner (John 5:24; 17:1-3; Eph. 2:1-10). It was God who gave the boy life, but He used Elisha as the means to do it. So it is with raising sinners from the dead: God needs witnesses, prayer warriors, and concerned saints to bring that life to them. Said Charles Spurgeon, "The Holy Ghost works by those who feel they would lay down their own lives for the good of others, and would impart to them not only their goods and their instructions, but themselves also, if by any means they might save some. O for more Elishas, for then we should see more sinners raised from their death in sin."[6]

Grace removes the curse (2 Kings 4:38-41)
Elisha visited the sons of the prophets at Gilgal during the time of the famine (8:1), and he commanded Gehazi his servant to make a stew for the men. Vegetables were scarce so some of the men went looking in the fields for herbs they could add to the stew. The student who came with a cloak filled with gourds wasn't knowledgeable about such matters but just brought whatever looked edible. In fact, nobody knew what these gourds were!

What were the evidences that there was poison in the pot? The bitter taste of the stew was perhaps the first clue, and the men probably suffered stomach pains and nausea. There had been death in the water at Jericho (2:19-22), and now there was death in the pot at Gilgal. It had been introduced innocently by a well-meaning student, but it had to be removed. But it was a time of famine and food was scarce. Elisha dropped some flour into the pot, and the Lord removed the poison from the stew.

As far as we know, there were no poisonous plants growing in the Garden of Eden. They showed up with the thorns and thistles after Adam sinned (Gen. 3:17-19). Today, there is a great deal of "death in the pot," for we live under the curse of the law of sin and death, and sin and death are reigning in this world (Rom. 5:14-21). But when Jesus died on the cross, He bore the curse of the law for us (Gal. 3:13), and for those who have trusted Christ, grace is reigning (Rom. 5:21) and they are "reigning in life" (Rom. 5:17). The sting of death has been removed (1 Cor. 15:50-57)!

Grace satisfies the hungry (2 Kings 4:42-44)
In the northern kingdom of Israel, there was no official temple dedicated to Jehovah, and many of the faithful priests and Levites had left apostate Israel and moved to Judah (1 Kings 12:26-33; 2 Chron. 11:13-17). Since there was no sanctuary to which the people could bring their tithes and offerings (Lev. 2:14; 6:14-23; 23:9-17; Deut. 18:3-5), they brought them to the nearest school of the prophets where they would be shared by people true to the Mosaic Law. The firstfruit offerings of grain could be roasted heads of grain, fine flour baked into cakes, or even loaves of bread. All of this would be most welcome to the sons of the prophets, and certainly the Lord honored the people who refused to bow down to the golden calves at Dan and Bethel.

There were one hundred hungry men in the group, and though the gifts the man brought were honored by the Lord, they couldn't feed all of the men adequately. The situation parallels that of Christ and the disciples (Matt. 14:13-21; 15:29-33, and parallels in the Gospels). Gehazi's question "How can I set this before a hundred men?" (v. 43, NIV) sounds like Andrew's question about the five loaves and two fish, "[H]ow far will they go among so many?" (John 6:9, NIV).

But Elisha knew that the Lord had this difficult situation well under His control. He commanded his servant to set out the bread and grain, and when Gehazi obeyed, there was not only plenty of food for everybody, but there was food left over. The Word of the Lord had announced and accomplished the impossible.

When our Lord fed the five thousand, He used the miracle as a backdrop for preaching a strong salvation message about the Bread of Life (John 6:25ff). Elisha didn't preach a sermon, but the miracle assures us that God knows our needs and meets them as we trust Him. Today we have freezers and supermarkets to supply us with food, and there are food banks to help those who are poor. But in Elisha's time, people prepared and consumed their food a day at a time. That's why Jesus taught us to pray, "Give us this day our daily bread" (Matt. 6:11). During his years in the wilderness as an exile, David depended on God's provision, and he was able to say, "I have been young, and now am old; yet I have not seen the righteous forsaken, nor his descendants begging bread" (Ps. 37:25, NKJV). Out of the riches of His grace, the Lord meets our every need.

THREE

2 KINGS 5:1–6:7

Three Men—Three Miracles

Elisha was a miracle-working prophet who ministered to all sorts of people who brought him all kinds of needs. In this section, we see Elisha healing a distinguished general, judging his own servant and helping a lowly student get back to work. It may seem a long way from the lofty head of the army to a lost axhead, but both were important to God and to God's servant. Like our Lord when He ministered here on earth, Elisha had time for individuals and he wasn't influenced by their social standing or their financial worth. "Casting all your care upon Him, for He cares for you" (1 Peter 5:7, NKJV).

But as important as the miracles are in this section, the theme of *ministry* is even more important. The Lord not only gave new life to Naaman, He also gave him a new purpose in life, a new ministry. He would return to Syria (Aram) as much more than a general, for now he was an ambassador of the true and living God of Israel. Naaman gained a new purpose in life, but, alas, Gehazi lost his ministry because of his covetousness and deception. When Elisha recovered the lost axhead, the student got back his "cutting edge," and his ministry was restored to him.

Naaman—ministry received (2 Kings 5:1-19)

The Prophet Elijah is named twenty-nine times in the New Testament while Elisha is named only once. "And many lepers were in Israel in the time of Elisha the prophet, and none of them was cleansed except Naaman the Syrian" (Luke 4:27, NKJV). Naaman was a Gentile and the commander of the army of an enemy nation, so it's no wonder the congregation in Nazareth became angry with the Lord, interrupted His sermon and carried Him out of the synagogue. After all, why would the God of Israel heal a man who was a Gentile and outside the covenant? He was an enemy who kidnapped little Jewish girls, and a leper who should have been isolated and left to die. These people knew nothing about the sovereign grace of God. Like Naaman, they became angry, but unlike Naaman, they didn't humble themselves and trust the Lord. Naaman's experience with Elisha illustrates to us the gracious work of God in saving lost sinners.

Naaman needed the Lord (vv. 1-3). The king of Syria was Ben Hadad II, and as commander of the army, Naaman was the number two man in the nation. But with all his prestige, authority, and wealth, Naaman was a doomed man because under his uniform was the body of a leper. It appears from verse 11 that the infection was limited to one place, but leprosy has a tendency to spread and if left unchecked, it ultimately kills. Only the power of the God of Israel could heal him.

Although Naaman didn't realize it, the Lord had already worked on his behalf by giving him victory over the Assyrians. Jehovah is the covenant God of Israel, but He is also Lord of all the nations and can use any person, saved or unsaved, to accomplish His will (see Isa. 44:28; 45:13; Ezek. 30:24-25). The Lord also did a gracious thing when He permitted Naaman to bring the captive Jewish girl into his house to be his wife's maid. The girl was a slave, but because she trusted the God of Israel, she was free. Even more, she was a humble witness to her mistress. Her words were so convincing that the woman told her husband and he in turn informed the king. Never underestimate the power of a simple witness, for God can take words from the lips of a child and carry them to the ears of a king.

Although there is no direct scriptural statement that leprosy is a picture of sin, when you read Leviticus 13, you can clearly see parallels. Like leprosy, sin is deeper than the skin (v. 3), it spreads (v. 7), it defiles (v. 45), it isolates (v. 46), and it is fit only for the fire (vv. 52, 57).

Seeking the Lord (vv. 4-10). Naaman couldn't leave Syria without the king's permission, and he also needed an official letter of introduction to Joram, king of Israel. After all, Syria and Israel were enemies, and the arrival of the commander of the Syrian army could be greatly misunderstood. Both Naaman and Ben Hadad wrongly assumed that the prophet would do whatever the king commanded him to do and that both the king and the prophet would expect to receive expensive gifts in return. For that reason, Naaman took along 750 pounds of silver and 150 pounds of gold, plus costly garments. The servant girl had said nothing about kings or gifts; she only pointed to Elisha the prophet and told her mistress what the Lord could do. Unsaved people know nothing about the things of the Lord and only complicate that which is so simple (1 Cor. 2:14). We aren't saved by bringing gifts to God, but by receiving by faith His gift of eternal life (Eph. 2:8-9; John 3:16, 36; Rom. 6:23).

This was King Joram's opportunity to honor the Lord and begin to build peace between Syria and Israel, but he failed to take advantage of it. Although 3:11 suggests that Joram and Elisha weren't close friends, the king did know who Elisha was and what he could do. He also surely knew that Israel's task was to bear witness to the godless nations around them (Isa. 42:6; 49:6). But Joram's concerns were personal and political, not spiritual, and he interpreted the letter as a declaration of war.[1] Alarmed by the thought, he impulsively tore his clothes, something that kings rarely did; but his mind was blinded by unbelief and fear and he didn't understand what the Lord was doing.

The prophet was in his home in the city of Samaria, but he knew what the king had said and done in his palace, for God hides from His servants nothing they need to know (Amos 3:7).

His message to Joram must have irritated the king, but at the same time Elisha was rescuing Joram from personal embarrassment and possible international complications. Yes, there was a king on the throne, but there was also a prophet in Israel! The king was helpless to do anything, but the prophet was a channel of God's power.

Elisha knew that Naaman had to be humbled before he could be healed. Accustomed to the protocol of the palace, this esteemed leader expected to be recognized publicly and his lavish gifts accepted with exaggerated appreciation, because that's the way kings did things. But Elisha didn't even come out of his house to welcome the man! Instead, he sent a messenger (Gehazi?) instructing him to ride thirty-two miles to the Jordan River and immerse himself in it seven times. Then he would be cleansed of his leprosy.

Naaman had been seeking help and now his search was ended.

Resisting the Lord (vv. 11-12). If Naaman began his journey at Damascus, then he had traveled over one hundred miles to get to Samaria, so another thirty miles or so shouldn't have upset him. But it did, for the great general became angry. The basic cause of his anger was pride. He had already decided in his own mind just how the prophet would heal him, but God didn't work that way. Before sinners can receive God's grace, they must submit to God's will, for "God resists the proud, but gives grace to the humble" (1 Peter 5:5, NKJV; see Rom. 10:1-3). Dr. Donald Grey Barnhouse used to say, "Everybody has the privilege of going to heaven God's way or going to hell their own way."

The Lord had already been working on Naaman's pride and there was more to come. King Joram wasn't able to heal him, the prophet didn't come to court or even come out to greet him, and he had to dip in the dirty Jordan River, not once but seven times. And he a great general and second in command over the nation of Syria! "Ah, that is just the trouble," said evangelist D. L. Moody when preaching on this passage. "He had marked out a way of his own for the prophet to heal him, and was mad because he didn't follow his plans." Is it any different today? People want to be saved from their sins by participating in a religious ritual, joining a church, giving money to the church, reforming their lives, doing good works, and a host of other substitutes for putting faith in Jesus Christ. "Not by works of righteousness which we have done, but according to his mercy he saved us" (Titus 3:5).

Naaman had another problem: he preferred the rivers back in Damascus to the muddy Jordan River.[2] He thought his healing would come from the water, so it was logical that the better the water, the better the healing. He would rather have his own way and travel over a hundred miles than obey God's way and go thirty-two miles! He was so close to salvation and yet so far away!

Trusting the Lord (vv. 13-15a). Once again, the Lord used servants to accomplish His purposes (vv. 2-3). If Naaman wouldn't listen to the command of the prophet, perhaps he would heed the counsel of his own servants. "Come now, and let us reason together, says the Lord" (Isa. 1:18). Elisha didn't ask him to do something difficult or impossible, because that would only have increased his pride. He asked him to obey a simple command and perform a humbling act, and it was unreasonable not to submit. When Naaman told his story back in Syria and got to this point, his friend would say, "You did what?" Faith that doesn't lead to obedience isn't faith at all.

When he came up from the water the seventh time, his leprosy was gone and his flesh was like that of a little child. In New Testament language, he was born again (John 3:3-8). "Assuredly, I say to you, unless you are converted and become as little children, you will by no means enter the kingdom of heaven" (Matt. 18:3, NKJV). By his obedience he demonstrated his faith in God's promise, and the Lord cleansed him of his leprosy. To quote D. L. Moody again, "He lost his temper; then he lost his pride; then he lost his leprosy; that is generally the order in which proud rebellious sinners are converted." Naaman gave a clear public testimony that the Lord God of Israel was the only true and living God and was the God of all the earth. He renounced the false gods and idols of Syria and identified himself with Jehovah.

What an indictment this testimony was against the idol-worshiping king and people of Israel!

Serving the Lord (vv. 15b-19). Like every new believer, Naaman still had a lot to learn. He had been saved and healed by trusting in God's grace, and now he had to grow in grace and faith and learn how to live to please the God who saved him. Instead of hurrying home to share the good news, Naaman returned to the house of Elisha to thank the Lord and His servant. (See Luke 17:11-19.) That meant traveling another thirty miles, but he must have rejoiced during the entire trip. It was natural for him to want to reward Elisha, but had the prophet accepted the gift, he would have taken the credit to himself and robbed God of glory. God saves us "to the praise of the glory of His grace" (Eph. 1:6, 12, 14). He also would have given Naaman, a new convert, the impression that his gifts had something to do with his salvation. Abraham had refused the gifts from the king of Sodom (Gen. 14:17-24), Daniel would refuse the king's offer (Dan. 5:17), and Peter and John would reject Simon's money (Acts 8:18-24).

Naaman was starting to grow in his understanding of the Lord, but he still had a long way to go. Elisha refused his gifts, but Naaman asked if he could take some native soil with him to Syria to use in his worship of Jehovah. In those days, people had the idea that the gods of a nation resided in that land, and if you left the land, you left the god behind. But Naaman had just testified that Jehovah was God in all the earth (v. 15)! However, taking that soil was a courageous act, because his master and his friends would surely ask Naaman what it meant, and he would have to tell them of his faith in the God of Israel.

In his second request, Naaman showed unusual insight, for he realized that the king would expect him to continue his official acts as the commander of the army. This included accompanying the king into the temple of Rimmon, the Syrian equivalent of Baal. Naaman was willing to perform this ritual outwardly, but he wanted Elisha to know that his heart would not be in it. Naaman anticipated that his healing and his changed life would have an impact on the royal court and eventually lead to the king's conversion. Instead of criticizing believers who serve in public offices, we need to pray for them, because they face very difficult decisions.[3]

It's interesting that Elisha didn't lecture him or admonish him but just said, "Go in peace." This was the usual covenant blessing the Jews invoked when people were starting on a journey. The prophet would pray for him and trust God to use him in his new ministry in Syria. Naaman's leprosy was gone, he still had the treasures, he carried soil from Israel, and he knew the true and living God. What a witness he could be in that dark land—and Naaman's servant girl would join him!

Gehazi—ministry revoked (2 Kings 5:20-27)
While Naaman was seeking to live the truth and please the Lord, Elisha's servant was wallowing in deception and unholy desires. "Thou shalt not covet" is the last of the Ten Commandments (Ex. 20:17), but when you break this one commandment, you tempt yourself to break the other nine. Covetous people will make idols out of material wealth, bear false witness, steal, dishonor God's name, abuse their parents, and even murder. Gehazi had been decaying in his spiritual life, and this was the climax. He had pushed away the woman whose son died (4:27), and he had no power to raise the boy to life (4:31). Now his covetousness took control, it led to lying, and it finally resulted in Gehazi becoming a leper. The disease on the outside typified the decay on the inside.

He lied to himself (v. 20). When he refused the gifts, Elisha hadn't been "easy" on Naaman but had taught the young believer a difficult lesson. Gehazi was measuring his master's conduct the way the world would measure it, not the way God measured it. Like our Lord's disciples when Mary anointed Jesus, he asked, "Why this waste?" (Mark 14:3-9), only in Gehazi's situation, it was a wasted opportunity to get wealth. He actually believed he would be a better and a happier man if he took some gifts from Naaman and that he had the right to do it. "Take heed and beware of covetousness, for one's life does not consist in the abundance of the things he possesses" (Luke 12:15, NKJV).

Surely Gehazi knew that Naaman's salvation and healing were wholly by the grace of God and that taking gifts might give the Syrian general the impression that he could do something to save himself. When he returned to Syria, Naaman would have to account for the missing treasures, and this could only weaken his testimony. Abraham refused gifts from the king of Sodom so he wouldn't compromise his testimony before the people of Sodom who needed to know the Lord (Gen. 14). Peter and John refused Simon's offer lest they give the Samaritans the idea that God's gifts could be purchased with money (Acts 8:20ff). The Apostle Paul even refused financial support from the church at Corinth lest the people think he was just another traveling philosopher, out to collect money.[4]

Gehazi took the Lord's name in vain when he said "As the Lord lives" (v. 20, see v. 16), for he had sin in his heart and was planning to sin even more. We get the impression that Gehazi had no fear of God in his heart and privately used God's name carelessly. Had he revered the name of God—the third commandment, Exodus 20:7—he would not have been controlled by greed.

He lied to Naaman (vv. 21-24). Naaman's caravan wasn't too far away and Gehazi was able to run and catch up with it (see 4:26, 29). Naaman did a noble thing when he stopped his chariot and stepped down to meet Elisha's servant. (See Acts 8:31.) Perhaps Elisha had another message for him, or perhaps there was a need to be met. For a Syrian general to show such deference to a Jewish servant was certainly an indication that God had wrought a change in his heart. Naaman greeted him with "Shalom—is all well?" and Gehazi replied "Shalom—all is well." But all wasn't well! When a man's heart is filled with greed and his lips are filled with lies, he is far from enjoying *shalom*, which means "peace, well-being, fulfillment, prosperity, safety."

In carrying out his evil plan, Gehazi not only used God's name in vain, but he also used God's work as a "cloak of covetousness"

(1 Thes. 2:1-6). Using Elisha's name, he lied to Naaman when he asked for gifts for two sons of the prophets from Bethel and Gilgal. These schools were located in the area of Mount Ephraim. We must not criticize Naaman for believing Gehazi's lies, for after all, he was a young believer and lacked the discernment that comes with a maturing spiritual experience. "My master has sent me" was a deliberate falsehood, although unknown to Gehazi, his master knew what he had done. Naaman not only gave Gehazi more than he requested and wrapped it neatly, but he also assigned two of his servants to carry the gifts for him. When the three men arrived at the hill on which Samaria was built (or perhaps a hill between them and Samaria), Gehazi took the bundle and sent the men back, lest somebody recognize them and start asking questions. Gehazi was near his master's house and he had to be careful not to let him know what he had done.

He lied to Elisha (vv. vv. 25-27). Acting very innocent, Gehazi went and stood

before his master, awaiting orders; but he found himself on trial! Gehazi had forgotten that "all things are naked and open to the eyes of Him to whom we must give account" (Heb. 4:13, NKJV). God knew what Gehazi had done and He communicated it to His servant. The scene reminds us of how Joshua interrogated Achan (Josh. 7) and Peter interrogated Ananias and Sapphira (Acts 5), all of whom had coveted wealth and lied about it.

Elisha not only saw what his servant had done, but he saw into his servant's heart and knew why he did it. Gehazi longed to be a wealthy man with land, flocks and herds, expensive clothing, and servants to obey his orders. He wasn't content to labor by the side of Elisha the prophet; he wanted to have security and comfort. There's certainly nothing wrong with being wealthy, if that's God's will for your life, for Abraham and Isaac were wealthy and so was David. But it is wrong to get that wealth through deceit and to make that wealth your god. Gehazi used the ministry God gave him as a means of deceiving Naaman, and that is contrary to God's will (1 Thes. 2:1-6; 2 Cor. 2:17; 4:2).

God judged Gehazi by giving him leprosy and promising that at least one of his descendants in each generation would be a leper. The covetousness that ate away at his heart became leprosy eating away at his body. Gehazi had hoped to leave great wealth to his descendants, but instead, he left great shame and sorrow for years to come. In Israel, lepers were considered unclean and weren't allowed to be in the community and live normal lives. Gehazi could no longer be Elisha's servant; he had lost his ministry. "Not greedy for money" is one of the qualifications for God's servants (1 Tim. 3:3). One of the marks of the last days is that people will love money more than they love God or other people (2 Tim. 3:1-5).

The student—ministry restored (2 Kings 6:1-7)
Elisha wasn't only a traveling preacher and a miracle-working prophet, but he was also the overseer of several schools of the prophets where young men called to ministry were trained and encouraged. We know there were schools in Gilgal, Bethel, and Jericho (2:1-5) and also in Samuel's hometown of Ramah (1 Sam. 19:22-24), but there may have been others. Both Elijah and Elisha were concerned that the next generation know the Lord and understand His Word, and this is the church's commission today (2 Tim. 2:2). D. L. Moody and Charles Spurgeon were not privileged to have formal training for ministry, but both of them started schools that are still training God's servants today. It's good to serve our own generation, but let's not forget the generations to come.

This account picks up the story from 4:44. God had blessed the school at Jericho and it was necessary to enlarge their quarters. The students studied together when the prophet visited them, for they met with him and sat before him to hear him teach (v. 1). They also ate together (4:38-44), but they lived in their own family dwellings (4:1-7). It's a good sign when God is raising up a new generation of servants and when the veteran ministers of God take time to teach them.

But new growth brings new obligations, and the facilities at

Jordan had to be enlarged. Schools today would do fund-raising and hire architects and contractors, but in Elisha's day, the students did the work. Not only that, but the leader of the school went with them and encouraged the work. Elisha had a shepherd's heart and was willing to go with his flock and share their burdens.

The Jewish people didn't have hardware stores stocked with tools such as we have today. Iron tools were precious and scarce, which explains why the student had to borrow an ax so he could help prepare the timber. (When I was in seminary, I didn't own any tools.) Not only were tools scarce, but they weren't constructed with the strength and durability of our tools today. In fact, Moses gave a special law relating to damage that might result when an axhead flew off the handle (Deut. 19:4-5), so it must have happened frequently. If the law of borrowed animals also applied to borrowed tools (Ex. 22:14-15), then that poor student would have to reimburse the lender for the lost axhead, and that would probably upset the budget for weeks to come. Without the axhead, the student couldn't work and that would add to somebody else's burdens. All in all, the sunken axhead caused a great deal of trouble.

The student was quick enough to see where it fell and honest enough to report the accident to Elisha. The Jordan isn't the cleanest river in the Holy Land (5:12) and it would be very difficult for anybody to see the axhead lying at the bottom. The prophet didn't "fish out" the axhead with a pole. He threw a stick into the water at the place where the axhead sank, and the Lord raised the iron axhead so that it floated on the surface of the river and could be picked up. It was a quiet miracle from a powerful God through a compassionate servant.

There are some spiritual applications that we can learn from this incident, and perhaps the first is that *whatever we have has been "borrowed."* Paul asked, "And what do you have that you did not receive?" (1 Cor. 4:7, NKJV), and John the Baptist said, "A man can receive nothing unless it has been given to him from heaven" (John 3:27, NKJV). Whatever gifts, abilities, possessions, and opportunities we have are from God, and we will have to give an account of them when we see the Lord.

This student lost his valuable tool *while he was serving the Lord.* Faithful service is important, but it can also be threatening, for we might lose something valuable even as we do our work. Moses lost his patience and meekness while providing water for the people (Num. 20:1-13), and David lost his self-control while being kind to his neighbor (1 Sam. 25:13). God's servants must walk carefully before the Lord and take inventory of their "tools" lest they lose something they desperately need.

The good news is that *the Lord can recover what we have lost and put us back to work.* If we lose our "cutting edge," He can restore us and make us efficient in His service. The important thing is to know that you have lost it, and when and where you have lost it, and honestly confess it to Him. Then get back to work again!

While we're on the subject of axes, Ecc. 10:10 offers some good counsel: "If the axe is dull and he does not sharpen its edge, then he must exert more strength. Wisdom has the advantage of giving success" (NASB). The modern equivalent is, "Don't work harder—work smarter." Wisdom tells a worker to sharpen the tool before the work begins. But our text from Kings reminds us further to make sure that the sharp axhead is firmly set into the handle. Don't work without a cutting edge and don't lose your cutting edge.

FOUR

The Battle Is the Lord's

"From our point of view, it would have been more logical for the Lord to appoint Elijah, the "son of thunder," to confront the enemy armies that invaded Israel; but instead, He appointed Elisha, the quiet farm boy. Elisha was like the "still small voice" that followed the tumult of the wind, the earthquake, and the fire (1 Kings 19:11-12), just as Jesus followed John the Baptist who had an ax in his hand. By declaring the righteousness of God and calling for repentance, Elijah and John the Baptist both prepared the way for their successors to minister, for without conviction there can be no true conversion.

As always in Scripture, the key actor in the drama is the Lord, not the prophet. By what he said and did, as well as by what he didn't do, Elisha revealed the character of the God of Israel to King Joram and his people. Jehovah is not like the idols of the nations (Ps. 115), for He alone is the true and living God.

The God who sees (2 Kings 6:8-14)
Whenever the Syrians planned a border raid, the Lord gave Elisha the information and he warned the king. Baal could never

47

have done this for King Joram, for idols have "Eyes . . . but they do not see" (Ps. 115:5, NKJV). The Lord sees not only the actions of people but also their thoughts (Ps. 94:11; 139:1-4) and their hearts (Prov. 15:3, 11; Jer. 17:10; Acts 1:24). Most of the people in the northern kingdom of Israel were unfaithful to the Lord, and yet in His mercy He cared for them. "Behold, He who keeps Israel shall neither slumber nor sleep" (Ps. 121:4, NKJV).

The king of Syria was sure there was a traitor in his camp, for the mind of the unbeliever interprets everything from a worldly viewpoint. Idolaters become like the gods they worship (Ps. 115:8) so Ben Hadad was as blind as his god Rimmon (5:18). However, one of Ben Hadad's officers knew what was going on and informed the king that the prophet Elisha was in charge of "military intelligence" and knew what the king said and did even in his own bedroom.

The logical solution then was to eliminate Elisha. Once again you see the ignorance of the king, for if Elisha knew every scheme the king planned for the border raids, surely he would know this scheme as well—and he did! Ben Hadad's spies found Elisha in Dothan, located about twelve miles north of the capital city of Samaria. Elisha's home was in Abel-meholah, but in his itinerant ministry, he moved from city to city. Humanly speaking, he would have been safer in the walled city of Samaria, but he had no fear, for he knew God was caring for him. The arrival that night of a company of foot soldiers, cavalry, and charioteers didn't upset the prophet in the least. This was not the full army but rather an enlarged "band" such as engaged in border raids (v. 23; 5:2; 13:20; 24:2).

When God's servants are in His will and doing His work, they are immortal until their work is done. The disciples tried to discourage Jesus from going back to Judah, but He assured them He was on a "divine timetable" and was therefore perfectly safe (John 11:7-10). It was only when His "hour had come" (John 13:1; 17:1) that His enemies had the power to arrest Him and crucify Him. If the Father's eye is on the sparrow (Matt. 10:29), then surely He is watching over His precious children.

The God who protects (2 Kings 6:15-17)

This servant was not Gehazi, for he had been removed and replaced. The young man was an early riser, which speaks well of him, but he was still deficient in his faith. Seeing the city surrounded by enemy troops, he did the normal think and turned to his master for help.

A woman told evangelist D. L. Moody that she had found a wonderful promise that gave her peace when she was troubled, and she quoted Psalm 56:3, "What time I am afraid, I will trust in thee." Moody said he had a better promise for her, and he quoted Isaiah 12:2, "Behold, God is my salvation; I will trust, and not be afraid." We wonder what promises from the Lord came to Elisha's mind and heart, for it's faith in God's Word that brings peace in the midst of the storm. Perhaps he recalled David's words in Ps. 27:3, "Though an army may encamp against me, my heart shall not fear; though war may rise against me, in this I will be confident" (NKJV). Or the words of Moses from Deuteronomy 20:3-4 may have come to mind, "Do not let your heart faint, do not be afraid . . . for the Lord your God is He who goes with you, to fight for you against your enemies, to save you" (NKJV).

Elisha didn't trouble himself about the army; his first concern was for his frightened servant. If he was going to walk with Elisha and serve God, the young man would face many difficult and dangerous situations, and he had to learn to learn to trust the Lord. We probably would have prayed that the Lord would give peace to the lad's heart or calmness to his mind, but Elisha prayed for God to open his eyes. The servant was living by sight and not by faith and couldn't see the vast angelic army of the Lord surrounding the city. Faith enables us to see God's invisible army (Heb. 11:27) and trust Him to give us the victory. Jacob had a similar experience before he met Esau (Gen. 32), and Jesus knew that, if His Father so desired, the angelic army could deliver Him (Matt. 26:53). "As the mountains surround Jerusalem, so the Lord surrounds His people" (Ps. 125:2 (NKJV). "The angel of the Lord encamps all around those who fear Him, and delivers them" (Ps. 34:7, NKJV). The angels are servants to God's people (Heb.

1:14), and until we get to heaven, we will never fully know how much they have helped us.

The God who shows mercy (2 Kings 6:18-23)
Elisha didn't ask the Lord to command the angelic army to destroy Ben Hadad's feeble troops. As with nations today, defeat only promotes retaliation, and Ben Hadad would have sent another company of soldiers. God gave Elisha a much better plan. He had just prayed that the Lord would open his servant's eyes, but now he prayed that God would cloud the eyes of the Syrian soldiers. The soldiers weren't made totally blind, otherwise they couldn't have followed Elijah; but their sight was clouded in such a way that they were able to see but not comprehend. They were under the delusion that they were being led to the house of Elisha, but Elisha was leading them to the city of Samaria!

When Elisha went out to meet the Syrian troops, did he lie to them (v. 19)? No, because he was no longer in the city of Dothan and was actually going to Samaria. The prophet was actually saving their lives, for if King Joram had been in charge, he would have killed them (v. 21). Elisha did bring the troops to the man they wanted. When the army arrived at Samaria, the guards must have been shocked to see the prophet leading the troops, but they obediently opened the gates and then God opened their eyes. Imagine their surprise when they found themselves at the heart of the capital city and at the mercy of the Israelites.

King Joram would have slain all of the Syrian soldiers and claimed a great victory for himself, but Elisha intervened. The king graciously called Elisha "my father" (v. 21), a term used by servants for their master (5:13), but later, he wanted to take off Elisha's head (vv. 32)! Like his wicked father Ahab, he could murder the innocent one day and then "walk softly" before the Lord the next day (1 Kings 21). Double-minded people are unstable (James 1:8).

Elisha's reply took the matter entirely out of the king's hands. Had Joram defeated this army in battle? No! If he had, he could kill his prisoners; but if he hadn't, then whoever captured the prisoners would decide what to do. These were not prisoners of war; they were Elisha's guests, so the king's responsibility was to feed them. Joram knew that having a meal with them was the same as making a covenant with them (Gen. 26:26-31), but he obeyed. In fact, he went beyond the prophet's request for bread and water and prepared a great feast for the soldiers.

Solomon wrote, "If your enemy is hungry, give him food to eat; if he is thirsty, give him water to drink. In doing this, you will heap burning coals on his head, and the Lord will reward you" (Prov. 25:21-22, NIV). In Romans 12:20-21, Paul quoted these words and applied them to believers today, and see also the words of Jesus in Matthew 5:43-48 and Luke 6:27-36. King Joram wanted to kill the Syrians, but Elisha "killed them with kindness." By eating together, they made a covenant of peace and the Syrian bands would no longer raid the borders of Israel.

Would this approach avert conflicts today? We must remember that Israel is a covenant nation and that the Lord fought their battles. No other nation can claim these privileges. But if kindness replaced long-standing and deeply rooted ethnic and religious differences among peoples, as well as national pride and international greed, there would no doubt be fewer wars and bombings. The same principle applies to ending divorce and abuse in families, riots and lootings in neighborhoods, uproars on campuses, and division and conflict in our communities. "Blessed are the merciful: for they shall obtain mercy" (Matt. 5:7).

The God who keeps His covenant (2 Kings 6:24-33)

The border raids stopped, but Ben Hadad II decided it was time again for war.[1] Rulers have to prove themselves to their people, and defeating and looting a neighbor is one of the best ways to reveal your strength and wisdom. This time he sent the full army and he seems to have caught Joram totally unprepared. Perhaps the peace along the borders lulled Joram into thinking that Syria was no longer a threat. Joram doesn't seem to have been very astute when it came to military matters.

The siege of Samaria lasted so long that the people in the city were starving. It seems that Elisha had counseled the king to wait (v. 33), promising that the Lord would do something, but the longer they waited, the worse the circumstances became. But it must be remembered that God warned that He would punish His people if they failed to live up to the terms of His covenant. Among His punishments were military defeat (Lev. 26:17, 25, 33, 36-39; Deut. 28:25-26, 49-52) and famine (Lev. 26:26, 29; Deut. 28:17, 48), and Israel was now experiencing both. Had King Joram called his people to repentance and prayer, the situation would have changed (2 Chron. 7:14). People were reduced to eating unclean food, such as a donkey's head and dove's droppings, and for these they paid exorbitant prices—two pounds of silver for the head and two ounces of silver for the dung.[2]

But even worse, people were eating their own children! This, too, was a predicted punishment for breaking God's covenant (Lev. 26:29; Deut. 28:53-57). King Joram met two such women as he walked on the wall and surveyed the city. One woman called to the king for help, and he thought she wanted food and drink. Joram's reply really put the blame on the Lord and not on the sins of the nation. God alone could fill the threshing floor and the winepress and provide food and drink. But the woman didn't want food and drink; she wanted justice. Her friend hadn't kept her part of the bargain but had hidden her son!

Joram was appalled that the nation had fallen so low, and he publicly tore his robe, not as a sign of sorrow and repentance but as an evidence of his anger at God and Elijah (see 5:7). When he did, he exposed the fact that he was wearing a rough sackcloth garment beneath the royal robe, but what good is sackcloth if there's no humility and repentance in the heart? His next words make it clear that he took no responsibility for the siege and the famine and that he wanted to murder Elisha. He even used the oath that he learned from his evil mother Jezebel (v. 31; 1 Kings 19:2). Joram's father Ahab called Elijah "the one who troubled Israel" (1 Kings 18:17), and Joram blamed Elisha for the plight Samaria was in at that time. The king sent a messenger to arrest

Elisha and take him out to be killed.

But the prophet wasn't upset or worried, for the Lord always told Elisha everything he needed to know. As the prophet sat in his house with the elders of the land, leaders who had come to him for counsel and help, he knew that the arresting officer was on his way. He also knew that the king himself would follow him to make sure the execution was a success. Elisha had already made it clear that he didn't accept the authority of the king of Israel because Joram was not of the line of David (3:14). Joram was the son of Ahab the murderer, the king who with his wife Jezebel killed the Lord's prophets who were opposing Baal worship (1 Kings 18:4). They also killed their neighbor Naboth so they could confiscate his property (1 Kings 21).

Elisha commanded the elders to hold the door shut until both men were outside. Being kept waiting at the door didn't help the king's temper one bit, and he called to Elijah, "It is the Lord who has brought this trouble on us! Why should I wait any longer for the Lord?" (v. 33, NLT). He should have said, "I am the cause of this great tragedy and I repent of my sins! Pray for me!" There was provision in the covenant for confession and forgiveness (Deut. 30) if only King Joram and his people had taken advantage of it. The Lord always keeps His covenant, whether to bless if His people obey or to discipline if they disobey.

The God who fulfills His promises (2 Kings 7:1-20)
Did Elisha and the elders allow the king to enter the room along with his attendant and messenger? They probably did, but Joram was a somewhat subdued man when the door was finally opened to him, not unlike his father Ahab when Elijah indicted him for the murder of Naboth (1 Kings 21:17ff). The only messages the Lord had sent to the rebellious King Joram were the army around the city and the starvation within the city, and the king still had not repented.

Good news from the Lord (vv. 1-2). How fortunate it was for the kingdom of Israel that they had Elisha the prophet living and ministering among them! Throughout Hebrew history, in times of crisis, the prophets had God's message for God's people, whether they obeyed it or not. King Joram could turn to the priests of Baal, but they had nothing to say. The Lord spoke through "his servants the prophets" (21:10)

Joram wanting something to happen now; he would wait no longer. But Elisha opened his message with "tomorrow about this time." What would happen? Food would once more be available and the inflationary prices would fall drastically. The fine flour for the people and the barley for the animals would cost about twice as much as in normal times. This was a great relief from the prices the people had paid for unclean food.

The officer who attended the king didn't believe the words of the prophet and scoffed at what Elisha said. "Will it become like Noah's flood," he asked, "with food instead of rain pouring out of heaven?" (See Gen. 7:11. The Hebrew word translated "windows" in the KJV means "floodgates.") To the humble heart that's open to God, the Word generates faith; but to the proud, self-centered heart, the Word makes the heart even harder. The same sun that melts the ice will harden the clay. The next morning, all the people in the city except this officer would awaken to life, but he would awaken to death.

Good news from the enemy camp (vv. 3-16). The scene shifts to outside the locked gates of Samaria where four lepers lived in isolation (Lev. 13:36). Nobody had told them about Elijah's promise of food. They were discussing their precarious situation when they came to an insightful conclusion: if they stayed at the gate, they would die of hunger, but if they went to the enemy camp, they might receive some pity and some food. Even if the Syrians killed them, it was better to die quickly from a sword's thrust than to die slowly from hunger. Lest they be observed from the city wall, they waited until twilight before going to the Syrian camp. Most of the camp would be resting and the lepers would have to deal only with some of the guards.

But nobody was there! The Lord had caused them to hear a sound which they interpreted as the coming of a vast army, and the Syrians had left their camp as it was and fled twenty-five miles to the Jordan River, scattering their possessions as they ran (v. 15). The Lord had defeated the Moabites by a miracle of sight (3:20-23) and now He defeated the Syrians by a miracle of sound. They thought the armies of the Egyptians and the Hittites were coming to destroy them.[3] The four lepers did what any hungry men would have done: they ate to the full and then looted the tents for wealth, which they hid.

However, as night came on, they stopped to have another conference and assess the situation. Why should an entire city be starving, and mothers eating their own children, while four dying men are selfishly enjoying the resources in the abandoned camp? Furthermore, when morning comes, the whole city will discover that the enemy has fled, and they'll wonder why the men didn't say something. When the truth comes out, the four men would be punished for keeping the good news to themselves.[4]

It was night when they found their way back to the city and approached the guard at the gate. Since these four men lived just outside the gate, the guards must have known them. The lepers gave him the good news and he shared it with the other guards, and one of the officers took the message to the king. Once again revealing his unbelief and pessimism (3:10, 13), Joram said that the whole thing was a trick, that the enemy was hiding and only trying to draw the people out of the city so they could move in. That was how Joshua had defeated the city of Ai (Josh. 8). It wasn't so much that he doubted the word of the lepers as that he rejected the word of Elisha. Had he believed the Word of the Lord, he would have accepted the good news from the lepers.

One of the officers had the good sense to reason with the king. Let some officers take a few horses and chariots and go investigate the terrain. If it all turns out to be a trick and they are killed, they would have died had they stayed in the city, so nothing is lost. The officer wanted five horses but the king let him have only two chariots with probably two horses per chariot. The men found the camp devoid of soldiers. Then they followed the escape route all the way to the Jordan River, a distance of twenty-five miles, and saw on the ground the clothing and equipment that the Syrians had discarded in their flight.

The spies raced back to the city and shared the good news that the Syrian army was gone and their camp was just waiting to be looted. It was indeed a day of good news as the people found food to eat and to sell back in the city, not to speak of valuable material goods that could be converted into cash. But the main lesson isn't that God rescued His people when they didn't deserve it, but that God fulfilled the promise He gave through His prophet Elisha. Note the emphasis on "the word of the Lord" in verses 16-18.

Jesus has promised to come again, but in these last days, people are questioning and even denying that promise. Fulfilling what Peter wrote in 2 Peter 3, the scoffers have now come and are asking, "Where is the promise of his coming?" The church is like those four lepers: we have the good news of salvation and we must not keep it to ourselves. If people don't believe the Word of the Lord, they won't be ready for His coming; but if we don't give them the message, they can't be ready for His coming. What will we say when we meet the Lord?

Bad news for the king's officer (vv. 17-20). It appears that this officer had gradually accepted the pessimistic unbelieving attitude of his king. To him, it was impossible for the prices to fall that low in one day and for fine flour and barley to be available so quickly. But God did it! The very people he thought would die of starvation came rushing out of the gate. They knocked him down, trod on his helpless body, and he died. The Word of the Lord lived on but the man who denied that Word was killed. "Heaven and earth will pass away," said Jesus, "but My words will by no means pass away" (Matt. 24:35, NKJV).

Jer 29:11, 13

FIVE

Reaping the Harvest of Sin

Eliphaz said some foolish things to his suffering friend Job, but he also stated some eternal principles, one of them being, "Even as I have seen, those who plow iniquity and sow trouble reap the same" (Job 4:8, NKJV). Solomon repeated this truth in Proverbs 22:8, "He who sows iniquity will reap sorrow" (NKJV), and the prophet Hosea put it graphically when he said, "They sow the wind, and reap the whirlwind" (Hos. 8:7, NKJV). Jeroboam, Omri, and Ahab had led the northern kingdom of Israel into idolatry, and Jehoram, who married a daughter of Ahab, had introduced Baal worship into the kingdom of Judah. Both kingdoms were rebellious against the Lord and polluted by idolatry, but now the day of judgment had arrived for Ahab's dynasty, the day that the Prophet Elijah had predicted (1 Kings 21:21, 29).

The greatness of God (2 Kings 8:1-6)
Obviously this event had to take place before the healing of Naaman (2 Kings 5), since the king wasn't likely to welcome a leper into the palace, and Gehazi was a leper (5:27). The author of 2 Kings doesn't claim to follow a strict chronology, and we're

not even sure which king Gehazi was entertaining with stories about his master. Perhaps this event occurred early in the reign of King Joram. This account reminds us of the greatness of the Lord. The events that follow reveal the sinfulness of people, but this section gives us a reminder that God is great and will accomplish His purposes in spite of the sinfulness of people, great and small.

God controls nature (8:1-2). We were introduced to the wealthy Shunamite woman and her family in 4:8-37. God often used famines to chasten His people when they were disobedient and needed to be reminded of their covenant obligations (Deut. 28:17, 48). This famine may have been the one mentioned in 4:38. The prophet warned the woman to escape the famine by going to the land of the Philistines and becoming a resident alien there. Knowing in advance that the famine was coming, she was able to secure a temporary home in Philistia ahead of the others who would flee Israel. Note that her husband isn't mentioned; but since he was older than she (4:14), it's likely he was dead.

This famine came because the Lord called for it, and He could command it because He is Lord of all. "Moreover He called for a famine in the land; He destroyed all the provision of bread" (Ps. 105:16, NKJV). In the beginning, God spoke and creation came into being (Gen. 1), and God speaks today and creation obeys His will (see Ps. 148). In these times of discipline and distress, if God's people would pray and confess their sins, God would have delivered them (2 Chron. 7:14). When people ignore God's Word, the Lord may speak through His creation and remind them who is in charge.

God controls life and death (8:3-5). The account of the miracles in the life of the Shunamite woman reveals the awesome power of God. She had no children and her husband was now old, but as with Abraham and Sarah (Gen. 17), the Lord gave them both new life and the woman conceived a son. But the son was struck with an illness and died, yet the Lord raised him from the dead. God keeps us among the living (Ps. 66:9), and "in his hand is the life of every creature and breath of all mankind" (Job 12:10, NIV).

"For in him we live, and move, and have our being" (Acts 17:28). Famines remind us that God alone can make nature fruitful, and death reminds us that God alone gives life and has the power and authority to take it away. "No one has power over the spirit to retain the spirit, and no one has power in the day of death" (Ecc. 8:8, NKJV).

God providentially controls the events in life (8:5-6). At the very moment Gehazi was describing this wonderful resurrection miracle, the mother of the child walked into the throne room! She had returned home only to discover that strangers had taken over her estate and robbed her of seven years' produce. In those days, it was common for people to bring such problems directly to the king and he would decide how property should be divided. The fact that Gehazi stood there as witness to her ownership of the land made it easy for the king to pass judgment. Years before, when her son had died, little did the mother realize that one day that bitter experience would play an important part in the preservation of her property.

Our English word "providence" comes from two Latin words, *pro* and *video*, which together mean "to see ahead, to see before." God not only knows what lies ahead; but He plans what is to happen in the future and executes His plan perfectly. Perhaps a better word is "prearrangement." In no way does God's providence interfere with our power of choice or our responsibility for the choices we make and their consequences. (See 1 Chron. 29:11; Job 41:11; Ps. 95:3-5; 135:6; 139:13-18; Dan. 4:35; James 4:13-15.)

This happy episode in the king's palace reveals to us the character of God and prepares us for the tumultuous events that follow. Hazael will murder Ben Hadad and become king of Syria. Jehu will sweep through the land and kill kings, princes, and pagan priests as he wipes out the house of Ahab and the worship of Baal. Evil Queen Jezebel and Queen Mother Athaliah will both meet their death and pay for their wicked deeds. What a time in history! Nevertheless, the Lord was on His throne, judging sin and fulfilling His Word. No matter what occurs in history, God is in control. He knows all things and can do all things. He is present everywhere, working out His will. He is a holy God who is longsuffering with sinners but eventually judges those who disobey Him. Our world may be shaking (Heb. 12:25-29), but our God can be trusted to do what is right.

The wickedness of the human heart (2 Kings 8:7-15)
When the Lord met with the Prophet Elijah on Mount Horeb (1 Kings 19:8-18), He gave him a threefold commission: to anoint Hazael king of Syria, to anoint Jehu king of Israel, and to anoint Elisha to minister as his successor (1 Kings 19:15-16). Before his translation to heaven, Elijah had fulfilled only one of those commissions, the anointing of Elisha (1 Kings 19:19-21), so we assume that he told Elisha to take care of the other two assignments. Jehu would become God's appointed scourge to rid the land of Ahab's evil descendants as well as Ahab's false religion.

The mission of Elisha (vv. 7-13). It took faith and courage for Elisha to travel to Damascus. After all, he had often thwarted Syria's plans for raiding Israel's border towns (6:9-12) and he had humiliated the Syrian army by leading them into Samaria and sending them home with full stomachs but empty hands (6:14-23). Because of Elisha, the Syrian army fled from Samaria and the Jewish people were able to loot their camp (7:1ff). But Elisha had also healed Naaman the Syrian of his leprosy (5:1ff), and when Elisha brought the Syrian raiding party to Samaria, he showed them mercy and saved their lives.

The fact that Ben Hadad the Syrian king was very ill and wanted help from the Lord made Elisha's arrival more significant. This was a pagan Gentile king seeking the help of a prophet of Jehovah, but perhaps the conversion of Naaman had something to do with it. Even more, Ben Hadad sent Hazael, one of his high officials, to meet Elisha and give him expensive gifts. The gifts were probably more like "bribes" and the king was hoping that his generosity would cause Elisha to give him a good answer. But like his master, Elisha undoubtedly refused to accept the gifts (5:15-16). By calling the king of Syria "your son," Hazael was seeking to add more honor to Elisha (see 6:21). Then he asked the key question: would the king of Syria recover from his sickness?

Elisha's reply appears to be deliberately ambiguous, for the Hebrew text can be read "You will certainly recover" or "Your will certainly not recover" (see NIV margin). The prophet seems to be saying, "The sickness will not take his life, but he will die by another means." In other words, the sickness was not terminal but the king's life was about to be terminated. As a high officer of the king, Hazael wanted to give the king good news, so he didn't convey to him the second part of the message. Elisha was not lying to Hazael. Hazael's question "Will the king recover from his sickness?" was answered "Yes and no." No, the sickness would not kill the king, but, yes, something else will kill him. However, Elisha didn't reveal what that "something else" was or when it would happen.

Elisha stared at Hazael, as though reading his mind and heart, and then the prophet broke into weeping. The Lord had shown him some of the violence and bloodshed that Hazael would perpetrate, brutal acts that were normal practices in ancient warfare (15:16; Hos. 13:16; Amos 1:3-5). Hazael's reply indicated that he recognized his subordinate status in the government and wondered where he would get the authority to do those things.[1] In calling himself "the dog," he wasn't referring to a vicious nature—"Am I some kind of dog that I would do these things?"—but rather that he was a nobody, a humble servant of the king, a man without such great authority. Elisha's reply stunned him: Hazael would have all the authority he needed because he would become king of Syria. The text doesn't tell us, but this may have been the point at which Elisha anointed Hazael with the sacred oil. If so, then Hazael was the only king of Israel, the Northern Kingdom, to have the anointing of the Lord.

Even before Elisha announced Hazael's great promotion, the prophet may have seen in Hazael's heart his plan to murder the king. Or, did the prophet's words stir up the desire in Hazael's heart? Either way, Elisha wasn't to blame for what Hazael decided to do. Hazael accepted the fact that he would be the next king, but he didn't ask how this would come about. Elisha made it clear that the king would die, but not because of his illness. "If the king is going to die anyway," Hazael might reason, "then why wait? Why not take his life now and become king much sooner?" When the human heart is bent on evil, it can invent all kinds of excuses. "The heart is more deceitful than all else and is desperately sick; who can understand it?" (Jer. 17:9, NASB).

When the king asked for Elisha's message, Hazael gave him the first half and said, "You will surely recover." In this, he told the truth, for the king would not die from his illness. But to make sure that the second half of the message was fulfilled, Hazael smothered him with a heavy wet cloth and seized the throne for himself. He ruled Syria for forty-one years (841–801 B.C.).

The foolishness of compromise (2 Kings 8:16-29; 2 Chron. 21)
The writer now shifts to the southern kingdom of Judah and tells us how King Jehoram brought apostasy and judgment to the land. For five years Jehoram served as coregent with his father Jehoshaphat, and when Jehoshaphat died, he took the throne. Jehoram was married to Athaliah, a daughter of Ahab, and Jehoshaphat had joined Ahab in fighting against the Syrians at Ramoth Gilead (1 Kings 22). In other words, the wall of separation was gradually crumbling between David's dynasty in Judah and the descendants of Ahab in Israel. The future of God's great plan of salvation depended on the continuation of the Davidic dynasty, so Jehoram was playing right into the enemy's hands. By compromising with the evil rulers of Israel, Jehoram displeased the Lord and weakened the nation.

A reign of terror (vv. 16-22). When he became king, Jehoram followed the example of Jezebel and murdered all his brothers and anybody who might threaten his authority (2 Chron. 21:1-7). His father had given each of the sons a fortified city to rule, and Jehoram didn't want them to unite against him. Instead of calling them together to pray and worship God at the temple and to seek His blessing, he followed the ways of Ahab and Jezebel and ruled by the sword. Jehoram wanted his brothers out of the way so they couldn't oppose his policy of promoting the worship of Baal. Jezebel had won again.

God could have destroyed the king and his kingdom, but for David's sake, He kept the dynasty alive (v. 19; see 1 Kings 11:36 and 15:4, and Pss. 89:29-37 and 132:17). But the Lord brought several defeats to Judah, including the revolts of Edom and Libnah (vv. 20-22; 2 Chron. 21:8-11). David had defeated and subdued Edom (2 Sam. 8:13-14; 1 Kings 11:15-17) but now they were free from Judah and put their own king on the throne. Jehoram's troops had invaded Edom but were surrounded by the army of Edom and barely broke through their lines to escape.

A word of warning (2 Chron. 21:12-15). We have noted before that the writer of 2 Kings didn't follow a strict chronology, and this is another instance. The translation of the Prophet Elijah to heaven is recorded in 2 Kings 2:11, but King Jehoram of Judah, son of Jehoshaphat, is mentioned in 1:17. This means that Elijah was alive and ministering during the early part of Jehoram's reign. We don't know how much time elapsed between the accession of Joram, king of Israel, and the events recorded in 2 Kings 2 that led up to the translation of Elijah. Writing this letter to the king of Judah may have been one of Elijah's last ministries.[2]

The prophet reminded Jehoram of three great kings of Judah: David, who founded the royal dynasty; Asa, a godly king who purged the land of evil (1 Kings 15:9-24; 2 Chron. 14–16); and Jehoram's father Jehoshaphat.[3] Instead of following in the ways of these kings, Jehoram patterned himself after Ahab. As a consequence, the people followed his bad example and it wasn't difficult for him to make Baal worship popular in Judah, the one place where Jehovah should have been worshiped without compromise.

Not only was Jehoram an idolater, but he was also a murderer and killed his own brothers; so the Lord would now cause him to reap what he had sown. The enemy would invade and loot the kingdom of Judah and take Jehoram's treasures as well as his wives and sons. Then, the king would be afflicted with an incurable bowel disease that would give his great pain and ultimately take his life. Both of these predictions came true. The Philistines and the Arabs invaded Judah, robbed the palace of its treasures, and took Jehoram's wives and sons, except for young Ahaziah, also known as Jehoahaz. The king contracted a painful lingering bowel disease and died after two years. But the people didn't mourn his death, nor did they stage the traditional "royal bon- fire" in his honor. But perhaps the most humiliating thing was that his body wasn't placed in a royal sepulcher, although he was buried in the city of David.[4]

Was Jehoram's compromise worth it? Of course not! "There is a way which seems right to a man, but its end is the way of death" (Prov. 16:25, NASB).

Unfortunately, he was followed by his son Ahaziah, who was also a follower of the Ahab clan, for his mother Athaliah was a daughter of Ahab.[5] Ahaziah joined with his uncle, King Joram, to take Ramoth Gilead from Hazael, king of Syria, and there Joram was wounded. He went to his palace at Jezreel to recover, and King Ahaziah went down to visit and encourage his uncle. Why does the writer give us these seemingly trivial details? To let us know that the Lord was putting together the people who would be slain because of their sins. "His going to Joram was God's occasion for Ahaziah's downfall" (2 Chron. 22:7, NKJV). To have the king of Judah and the king of Israel together in one place would make it easy for Jehu to obey the commandment of the Lord.

The suddenness of opportunity (2 Kings 9:1-13)
The scene now shifts to Ramoth Gilead where Israel and Judah had combined their forces to recover the city from the Syrians. One of the key commanders of the Israeli army was Jehu, the son of Jehoshaphat, but not the Jehoshaphat who was king of Judah and the father of Jehoram. Unknown to Jehu, the Prophet Elisha had dispatched one of the young sons of the prophets to anoint him king of Israel. This was the third assignment God gave Elijah (1 Kings 19:15-16). Instead of going to the battlefield himself, Elisha wisely gave the young man the authority to anoint Jehu

privately. Elisha advised the student to flee the scene as fast as he could, for obviously there was going to be serious conflict.

Jehu was having a staff meeting in the courtyard when the young man approached and asked for a private audience with the commander. They went into a private room in the house and there the young man anointed Jehu to be the new king of Israel. It's interesting that the young prophet called the people of Israel "the people of the Lord" (9:6). Even though Israel and Judah were separate kingdoms and not obedient to the covenant, the people were still the chosen ones of the Lord and Abraham's descendants. God's covenants with Abraham (Gen. 12:1-3) and with David (2 Sam. 7) would still stand. The people had turned away from the Lord, but He had not forsaken them.

The young man didn't end his work with the anointing but went on to explain to Jehu the work God wanted him to do. His main task was to wipe out the family of Ahab in Israel and execute God's judgment upon them because of the innocent people they had killed. He specifically mentioned Jezebel's crimes and her judgment, referring to the words Elijah spoke when he confronted Ahab (1 Kings 21:21-24). That prophecy may have been forgotten by Ahab's descendants, but God remembered it, and the time had come to fulfill it. Just as God had wiped out the descendants of Jeroboam and Baasha (1 Kings 15:25–16:7), He would use Jehu to destroy the house of Ahab.

The officers in the courtyard must have wondered who the young man was and why his message to Jehu was so confidential. Did he come from the front? Would there be a change in the battle plan? When the young man ran out of the house and fled, the officers were sure he was out of his mind. More than one servant of God has been accused of madness, including Paul (Acts 26:24; 2 Cor. 5:13) and Jesus (Mark 3:20-21, 31-35; John 10:20). Actually, it's the lost world that is mad and God's people who are the sane ones.

Was it a mark of humility in Jehu that he didn't immediately announce that he was king? The officers had to pull the truth out of him, but once they knew, they accepted their commander's promotion and openly acknowledged it. As far as the biblical record is concerned, Jehu is the only king of Israel who was anointed by an appointed servant of the Lord. Jehu's opportunity came suddenly, but he accepted it by faith and immediately began to serve the Lord. A Chinese proverb says, "Opportunity has a forelock but not a pigtail. Once it is past, you cannot grasp it." As the tenth king of Israel, Jehu started a new dynasty and reigned for twenty-eight years (10:36).

The swiftness of God's judgment (2 Kings 9:14-37; 2 Chron. 22:1-9)

Here is the situation as Jehu began his crusade. Ahaziah was reigning in Judah and following the counsel of his wicked mother Athaliah and the leaders in the house of Ahab in Israel. Baal was his god and he had no interest in the law of the Lord. Ahaziah had gone to Jezreel to visit King Joram, who was recovering from wounds received at Ramoth Gilead and did not know that God had given Israel a new king. Jehu wanted to catch his enemies by surprise, so he ordered his officers not to spread the word that he was king.

The death of Joram (vv. 16-26). It was about forty-five miles from Ramoth Gilead to Jezreel, but Jehu was a fast and daring charioteer and his men were accustomed to traveling at speeds that were alarming in those days. The word "peace" (shalom) is repeated eight times in this section (vv. 17-19, 22, 31), but the event was actually a declaration of war. Without slowing his pace, Jehu received Joram's two messengers and commanded them to ride with his company, and they obeyed. However, when his two messengers failed to return to Jezreel, Joram became suspicious and ordered his own chariot to be readied for an escape.

In a move that made Jehu's work much easier, Joram and Ahaziah each mounted his royal chariot and rode out to meet the man who had now been identified as Jehu. Perhaps the two kings were hoping that Jehu was bringing good news from the front. Joram's question "Have you come in peace?" might have meant "Has the battle at Ramoth ended in our favor?" or "Is your mission one of peace?" If it was the latter, it suggests that Jehu might have been somewhat of a "loose cannon" in Joram's army, and perhaps Joram suspected he had designs on the throne. Jehu's reply[6] instantly told the king that danger was in the air, and he tried to get away. Joram warned his nephew Ahaziah, who did escape but was later caught, but one well-directed arrow ended the life of Joram. As a patient recuperating from wounds, Joram wouldn't be wearing his armor. Providentially, he died on the property of Naboth that Ahab and Jezebel had taken after killing Naboth and his sons. Thus the Lord fulfilled the prophecy He gave to Elijah (1 Kings 21:18-24).

Jehu not only executed the king of Israel, but he also killed all the royal princes (2 Chron. 22:8).

The death of Ahaziah (vv. 27-29; 2 Chron. 22:1-9). The reports of Ahaziah's death in 2 Kings 9:27-29 and 2 Chronicles 22:7-9 aren't easy to harmonize, but we suggest a scenario. Ahaziah was wounded as he fled from Jezreel (v. 27). He made it to Beth-haggan and then turned northwest at the Ascent of Gur and headed for Megiddo where he tried to hide from Jehu. But Jehu's men tracked him down and killed him at Megiddo. Ahaziah's servants carried his body from Megiddo to Jerusalem where he was buried with the kings, for he was a descendant of David. Had he not compromised with Joram, worshiped Baal, and followed his mother Athaliah's counsel, he would have been spared all this shame and defeat.

The death of Jezebel (vv. 30-37). It didn't take long for Jezebel and the palace residents to hear that Jehu was in Jezreel, that he was king and that he had killed her son Joram. She put on her makeup, "attired her head," and watched at an upper window, waited for him to show up. When she saw him come through the gate, she called, "Is it well, Zimri, your master's murderer?" (v. 31, NASB). About fifty years before, Zimri had killed King Elah and made himself king and then had proceeded to exterminate the family of Baasha (1 Kings 16:8-20). Since Zimri ruled for only seven days and then died a suicide, Jezebel was obviously trying to warn Jehu that his authority was weak and his days were numbered. She might even have been suggesting that Jehu form an alliance with her and strengthen his throne.

But Jehu knew his mandate from the Lord. When he called for evidence of loyalty from the palace personnel, two or three servants responded, and they threw Jezebel out the window to the courtyard below. Jehu rode his horse over her body until he was sure she was dead. Since he was now king, Jehu went into the palace and called for something to eat. As he was dining, he remembered that, evil as she was, Jezebel was a princess, the daughter of Ethbaal, the Sidonian ruler (1 Kings 16:29-31); so he ordered the servants to bury her body. But it was too late. Smelling human blood, the wild dogs showed up and ate her body, leaving only her skull, feet and the palms or her hands. It was a gruesome scene, but it was what Elijah had predicted would happen (1 Kings 21:21-24). God's Word never fails but accomplishes His purposes on the earth (Isa. 55:10-11).

SIX

2 KINGS 10–11
[2 CHRONICLES 22:10–23:21]

The Sword and the Crown

Studying these two chapters gives you the feeling that you're reading the morning paper or watching the ten o'clock news on television. You meet two leaders—Jehu, former army commander and now ruler of the northern kingdom of Israel; and Jehoiada, high priest at the temple in Jerusalem in the Southern Kingdom. As you watch these two men, you recognize the fact that the same forces for good and for evil were at work in their world that are at work in our own world today.

You also recognize the difference between leaders who are motivated by selfish ambition and leaders who are motivated by spiritual dedication. Jehu was proud of his "zeal for the Lord" (10:16), but that "zeal" was a pious cloak that hid the egotism and anger that really motivated his service. God gave Jehu an important work to do, but the king went beyond the assigned boundaries and carried his mandate too far. The Lord commended Jehu for what he accomplished (10:30), but He also chastened him for his pride and compromise. Humanly speaking, were it not for the courageous service of the high priest Jehoiada and his wife Jehosheba, the Davidic dynasty would have come to an end. The future of God's promises to David, that involved His great plan of salvation, was all wrapped up in a little baby boy named Joash.

Let's identify the forces that were at work in that day, forces that are still at work in our world today,

1. Fear and double-talk (2 Kings 10:1-10)

Years before, Elijah had prophesied that the line of godless King Ahab would come to an end and that every last descendant of Ahab would be slain (1 Kings 21:20-29). The Lord gave this mission to Jehu when He anointed him king of Israel (2 Kings 9:6-10). Even though the nation was divided into two kingdoms, the Jews were still God's covenant people and their kings couldn't do whatever they pleased. Ahab and Jezebel had promoted Baal worship in Israel, and when Jehoram, king of Judah, married Athaliah, a daughter of Ahab, he encouraged Baal worship in Judah (8:16-18). By this evil marriage, Jehoram not only corrupted Judah with idol worship, but he corrupted the line of David and jeopardized the fulfillment of the messianic promises.

Jehu had already killed Joram, king of Israel, and Ahaziah, king of Judah (9:14-29), and he had also slain Jezebel, the evil wife of Ahab (9:30-37). Now Jehu was on a "search and destroy" mission to find and kill every one of Ahab's descendants. His first challenge was to get control of the capital city of Samaria where Ahab's male descendants were being protected and prepared for places of leadership in the government. Jehu knew that his forces couldn't easily take a walled city like Samaria, but being a clever strategist, he knew how to get his enemies to surrender. Once he had taken Samaria, the other key cities in the land would also surrender.

Samaria accepts Jehu's rule (vv. 1-5). Jehu was in Jezreel (9:30), about twenty-five miles north of Samaria, and from there, he communicated with the leaders in Samaria—the palace administrators, the military leaders, and the tutors and guardians of the princes. He knew that if he could intimidate these respected leaders, he could take over the city without a fight. His first challenge was that they choose one of Ahab's male descendants, put him on the throne and then defend his right to reign. This was probably a suggestion that the new king or a champion of his choice fight Jehu one-on-one and the winner take all. (See 1 Sam. 17:8ff and 2 Sam. 2:9.)

Jehu even pointed out their advantages: they were in a walled city and they had armor and weapons as well as chariots and horses. Jehu was using a technique that revolutionaries have used successfully for centuries: making a bold proposal and letting the leaders' imaginations create fear in their hearts. Adolf Hitler wrote, "Mental confusion, contradiction of feeling, indecisiveness, panic: these are our weapons." Three different groups of leaders had to unite on this decision, and these men knew that Jehu had killed two kings and disposed of Jezebel. Furthermore, he seemed invincible, for nobody had stood in his way. The message they sent to Jehu at Jezreel was one of complete unconditional surrender. They promised to do whatever he commanded and they agreed not to name a new king. In short, they accepted Jehu as their king.

Samaria obeys Jehu's orders (vv. 6-10). Now Jehu shows himself to be the master of political double-talk. He accepted their submission to his rule and then ordered them to "take the heads" of the seventy descendants of Ahab and bring them to Jezreel. This could mean "bring the leaders among the group to me and we'll discuss matters," or it could mean "behead all seventy and bring me their heads." It was the second interpretation that the leaders followed, so they immediately killed Ahab's descendants and sent messengers to Jezreel with the heads. When they arrived that evening, Jehu ordered the messengers to stack up the heads at the entrance of the city, certainly a grisly reminder to the people of Jezreel that it didn't pay to get in Jehu's way.

But the next morning, Jehu again showed himself a master politician by absolving himself of any guilt! He admitted that he had killed Joram, the former king of Israel, but since he had not left Jezreel, he couldn't have murdered the seventy young men. Then he reminded them of the divine promise that all of Ahab's descendants would be eliminated, so the responsibility ultimately lay with the Lord and His prophet Elijah. In one brief speech, Jehu washed his hands of the mass murder and also allied himself with the Lord and the Prophet Elijah!

Jehu practiced what is today called "double-speak." Taxes are now "revenue enhancement" and potholes are "pavement deficiencies." People are no longer bald; they are only "follicularly deprived." Hospital technicians gave a fatal dose of nitrous oxide to a mother about to deliver and killed both the mother and the child. They called the tragedy "a therapeutic misadventure." Poor people are now "fiscal underachievers" and soldiers no longer kill the enemy, they "service the target." David was right when he wrote, "They speak falsehood to one another; with flattering lips and with a double heart they speak" (Ps. 12:2, NASB).

Selfish ambition (10:11-17)

Jehu's divine commission had now become a personal crusade, motivated by his own selfish ambition. Novelist Joseph Conrad wrote in the preface to Some Reminiscences, "All ambitions are lawful except those which climb upward on the miseries and credulities of mankind." Lawful ambition used truth and builds on the past, while unlawful ambition uses lies and destroys the past. Dictators must annihilate their enemies in order to be safe, but in so doing, they destroy the past and the information and help they need for moving into the future. A German aphorism says, "Every eel hopes to become a whale," and Jehu was now driving in that lane.

He goes too far (vv. 11-14). To prove that he intended to obey God and purge the land of Ahab's family, Jehu proceeded to kill all of Ahab's descendants that he found in Jezreel. But he didn't stop there; he went beyond his divine commission and killed Ahab's close friends, his chief officers, and the priests who served in the palace. It was a wholesale slaughter based on "guilt by association." The Lord wanted to rid the land of Ahab's family so that none of them could usurp the throne, but for Jehu to kill Ahab's friends, officers, and priests was totally unnecessary. In fact, Jehu later had serious problems with the Syrians (10:22-23) and could have used some of the wisdom and experience of the court officers he killed. By wiping out these former leaders, Jehu destroyed a valuable source of political wisdom and skill.

He then left Jezreel and went to Samaria to claim his throne. On the way, he met a group of travelers who were going to Jerusalem to visit King Ahaziah, who was related to them. They didn't know that King Ahaziah, King Joram, and Queen Jezebel were all dead and that Jehu had killed them and was now in charge. Since Ahaziah had married into Ahab's family (8:18), it seemed logical to Jehu that anybody related to Ahaziah belonged to the enemy, so he had all forty-two men slain. But these men weren't related by blood to Ahab; they were descendants of David! Jehu was now attacking the Davidic dynasty! (See 2 Chron. 22:8.)

He enlists a friend (vv. 15-17). Jehu now encountered an ally, Jehonadab the Rechabite, and used him to give respectability to his own ambitions. The Rechabites were a people that belonged to the Kenites, the descendants of Moses' brother-in-law Hobab (Jud. 4:11). They identified with the tribe of Judah (Jud. 1:16) but stayed to themselves and followed the traditions laid down by their ancestors (Jer. 35). They were respected highly by the Jewish people, but, being nomads and tent-dwellers, the Rechabites were separated from the everyday city life and politics of the Jews.

Jehonadab was just the kind of man Jehu needed to make his crusade look credible. When Jehonadab took Jehu's hand and stepped into the royal chariot, he declared that he was heart and soul behind the new king. Certainly Jehonadab disapproved of Baal worship and rejoiced to hear that Ahab's family was being eradicated. However, when he met Jehu, Jehonadab didn't know the motives that were driving the king and the ruthless methods he was using.

Every ambitious leader needs a respectable second man to help "sell" his policies and practices to the public. It was bad enough that Jehu had begun to murder innocent people, but now he was "using" an innocent man to make his crimes look like the work of the Lord. However, this is the way many unscrupulous leaders operate. Jehu's statement "see my zeal for the Lord" (v. 16) reminds us of the words of Elijah when he was running from Jezebel and hiding in the cave (1 Kings 19:10, 14). The Hebrew word can be translated "jealous" or "zealous."

When Jehu and Jehonadab arrived at Samaria with the company of soldiers, Jehu presented himself as their king and the people submitted to him. Jehu had already intimidated the rulers of the city, so he met no opposition when he rode through the city gate. The city officers turned Ahab's remaining relatives over to him and Jehu killed them all.

Deception (2 Kings 10:18-28)

Jehu had finished the work of ridding the nation of Ahab's family, so there were no descendants who could challenge his right to the throne. But what about the Baal worship that had infected the land? That was Jehu's next responsibility and he decided to use deception as his major weapon.

As king of Israel, Jehu could have dealt with the Baal worshipers in one of three ways. He could have commanded them to leave the land, or he could have obeyed Deuteronomy 13 and killed them. He might even have tried to convert them, although it would have been easy to "convert" if the sword was hanging over your head. He also could have ordered the temple of Baal to be torn down. Jehu had the promised support of the leaders in Samaria (v. 5), so why did he choose to lie to the people and then kill them? God's servants are not allowed to "do evil that good may come" (Rom. 3:8, NASB; see 1 Thes. 2:3), yet that's the course that Jehu took. He had authority from Moses to kill the idolaters, and that he did; but why did he deceive them first?

He lied to them about himself, claiming that he was more devoted to Baal than Ahab had been. He also lied about the service in the temple of Baal. However, this may have been another instance of Jehu's "double-speak," for there *was* a "great sacrifice" to Baal—the lives of the priests and the worshipers in Baal's temple! Jehu was a military man whose life was so dedicated to strategy and conquest that, unlike David, he couldn't bring faith and the glory of God into his battles. Jehu seems to have had a lust for blood and a joy in outsmarting his enemies, and we never read that he sought the mind of the Lord in any of his endeavors.

First, he assembled the prophets, ministers, and priests of Baal and commanded them to announce a great sacrifice for Baal. Coming from the king through the religious leaders, the announcement would carry much more weight and be more believable. Jehu even sent messengers throughout the land to command the Baal worshipers to attend the great sacrifice in Samaria. The house of Baal in Samaria was built by Ahab for Jezebel (1 Kings 16:31-32), so Jehu would destroy "the house of Ahab" in two senses: his physical "house" or family and the house he built for Baal.

Once the people were in the temple, Jehu made sure that no true worshipers of Jehovah were among the worshipers of Baal. He commanded that the Baal worshipers wear the special garments that were used during their services, and he and Jehonadab admonished the priests not to allow any outsiders to participate (v. 23). Jehu gave the impression that he wanted "pure worship" for the great sacrifice. Once the Baal worshipers were ready inside the temple, Jehu instructed his eighty soldiers outside the temple to be ready to enter the temple as soon as the sacrifice was ended.

Does the "he" in verse 25 (KJV) refer to Jehu or to the high priest of Baal? The NIV and the NASB both opt for Jehu, but not knowing the layout of the temple or the order of the service, it's difficult to decide. How could the king be visible at the altar and, without raising suspicion, leave the altar and go outside to command the soldiers? It's likely that Jehu provided the animals for the sacrifices, so in that sense, *he* was "sacrificing to Baal" whether he was at the altar or not. The soldiers killed all the Baal worshipers in the temple and threw their bodies outside into the court. Then some of the men went into the inner shrine of the temple and removed the wooden images of the gods and the stone image of Baal and destroyed them. What once was the sacred house of Baal was turned into a public latrine.

Jehu's plan worked and enabled him in one day to wipe out Baal worship in the land. By lying to the people, he accumulated a larger crowd of Baal worshipers than if he had gone after them one by one, but it's unfortunate that his first public act as king in Samaria was an act of deception. Would anybody trust him after that?

Compromise (2 Kings 10:29-36)
Once things quieted down, Jehu had a long reign of twenty-eight years; but he followed the ways of Jeroboam and worshiped the golden calves at Dan and Bethel. The calves were supposed to be only symbols of Jehovah, but it was idolatry just the same. In spite of his zeal for the Lord, Jehu was an idolater at heart who used the Lord's name only to cover up his sins. By being a part of the "national religion," Jehu united the people and gained their respect. Jehu was a consummate politician to the very end.

The Lord commended Jehu for the work he had done and rewarded him by giving him the longest dynasty in the history of the Northern Kingdom—over one hundred years. He was succeeded by Jehoahaz, Joash, Jeroboam II and Zechariah, all of whom were bad kings. But the Prophet Hosea announced that the Lord was displeased with Jehu for murdering innocent people (Hos. 1:4; 2:21). Jehu established his dynasty by killing King Joram at Jezreel (2 Kings 9:15ff), and for this God would judge him. "Jezreel" means "God scatters" and He would scatter the Northern Kingdom by allowing the Assyrians to conquer them in 722 B.C. Jehu's great-great-grandson Zechariah reigned only six months and was assassinated by Shallum who reigned only one month. The dynasty began with a murder and ended with a murder.

Even during Jehu's lifetime, the Lord chastened him by allowing Israel's old enemy Syria (Aram) to take territory from the tribes east of the Jordan. Having the enemy living right across the Jordan River wasn't a comfortable situation for the nation. Jehu was an effective soldier but he wasn't much of a builder, and he's remembered only for the people he killed. He could have assembled a group of gifted men to assist him in promoting the true faith in the land, but he settled for following the crowd and worshiping the golden calves.

Retaliation (2 Kings 11:1; 2 Chron. 22:10)
We move now to the southern kingdom of Judah where the throne was empty because Jehu had killed King Ahaziah near Jezreel (9:27-28). The queen mother Athaliah, a daughter of Ahab, saw her opportunity and seized the throne, reigning for six years. As the founder of Baal worship in Judah, she had no desire to see the Davidic dynasty succeed. She tried to kill all the royal princes, but one survived. David's family was rapidly being destroyed. When Jehoram became king of Judah, he killed all his brothers and some of the princes of Israel to prevent them from dethroning him (2 Chron. 21:4), and the Arabian invaders had killed Jehoram's older sons (22:1). Jehu had killed some of David's descendants (22:8), and now Athaliah had ordered the "royal seed" to be wiped out. Satan certainly did his utmost to keep the promised Messiah from being born in David's family in Bethlehem!

Athaliah was retaliating because of all that Jehu had done in eradicating Ahab's family and Baal worship in Israel. To return evil for good is demonic; to return good for evil is godlike; and to return evil for evil and good for good is human. Wherever there is conflict in this world, you will usually find this spirit of revenge and retaliation. As individuals used to fight duels to uphold their personal honor, so nations sometimes fight wars to protect their national honor. But by killing the royal seed, Athaliah was rebelling against the Lord Jehovah who had promised David that he would have a descendant sitting on his throne in Jerusalem.

Most of us don't go to that extreme in seeking to "pay back" our enemies, but revenge isn't an unknown thing among God's people. Moses in the law admonished his people not to practice revenge (Lev. 19:18), and Solomon gave the same counsel (Prov. 20:22; 24:29). Jesus taught against personal revenge (Matt. 5:38-48), as did the apostles Paul (Rom. 12:17-21) and Peter (1 Peter

3:8-9). Planning and executing revenge does far more harm to the perpetrator than to the victim. Many famous authors have written about "sweet revenge," but experience shows that revenge is very bitter. A Jewish proverb says, "The smallest revenge will poison the soul." If you are going to pay back an enemy, choose a good one, because paying back an enemy is a very expensive luxury.

Faith and courage (2 Kings 11:2-12; 2 Chron. 22:11–23:11).
When wicked Athaliah killed the heirs to David's throne, the faithful remnant in Judah must have wondered where God was and what He was doing. Why would He make a covenant promise to David and not keep it? How could He allow the queen mother to do such an evil deed and jeopardize the future of the messianic line? But God was still on the throne and had His servants prepared to act. In a world that seems to be controlled by deceit and selfish ambition, there are still people like Jehoiada and Jehosheba who have faith in God's Word and courageously do His will.

Protection (vv. 2-3; 22:11-12). Jehoiada was the high priest and Jehosheba his wife was a princess, a daughter of King Jehoram and a sister to King Ahaziah, whom Jehu had slain. This made her an aunt to little Joash. That such a godly woman should come out of that family is a miracle of the grace of God. Knowing what Athaliah planned to do, the priest and the princess stole one-year-old Joash from the royal nursery and hid him with his nurse, first in a room where old bedding was stored and then in a room in the temple. As he grew older, he mingled and played with the other children in the temple area and wasn't recognized as an heir to the throne.[1]

Presentation (vv. 4-12; 23:1-11). Jehoiada and Jehosheba and the boy's nurse had the patience to wait for God's time, for faith and patience go together (Heb. 6:12). "Whoever believes will not act hastily" (Isa. 28:16, NKJV). In His gracious providence, the Lord watched over the child as well as the three people who knew who he was and where he was; for if Queen Athaliah had known what they were doing, she would have killed them along with the prince.

While waiting those six years, the high priest had thought and prayed and the Lord told him how to take Athaliah off the throne and put Joash on the throne. First, he called together the five officers who were in charge of the temple guard, presented the king to them and had them take an oath to obey his orders and tell no one what was going to transpire. After outlining his plan, he sent them throughout the kingdom of Judah to order the Levites living away from Jerusalem and the heads of the Jewish families (clans) to come to Jerusalem on a specific Sabbath day. They were to assemble at the temple as though they were there to worship the Lord.

Jehoiada's plan was simple but effective. The five officers each commanded one hundred men. Two companies would ordinarily be on duty daily and be replaced on the Sabbath Day, but on this particular Sabbath they would remain on duty and guard the king. A third company would guard the palace where Athaliah lived, and this would give her a false sense of security. A fourth company was assigned to the gate Sur (or "the foundation gate"—23:5), which may have led from the nearby palace to the temple area. The fifth company assembled at the gate behind the guardhouse, a normal place for the temple guards to gather. Anybody watching at the temple would have no reason to suspect that anything dramatic was about to occur. They would see the guards march in and take their usual places, and they might notice that the crowd of worshipers in the temple was larger than usual.

Even King David was involved in the plan! The high priest distributed to the men the weapons that David had confiscated in his many battles, and the guards protected David's own heir with those weapons. It was David who purchased the property on which the temple stood (2 Sam. 24:18ff), and it was David who provided the wealth that enabled Solomon to build the temple. Some of it came from his own personal treasury and the rest from the spoils of the battles he had fought for the Lord (1 Chron. 28–29). He wrote many of the songs the Levites sang in the temple services, and now he was providing the weapons to defend his own dynasty. David not only served his own generation (Acts 13:36) but every generation that followed. What an example for us to follow!

When everybody was in place, Jehoiada brought out the seven-year-old king and presented him to the people. Jehoiada put the crown on Joash's head and gave him a copy of the law of God that he was to obey (Deut. 17:14-12; 31:26). The high priest anointed him and the people joyfully welcomed him as their ruler. "God save the king" is literally "Let the king live!" (See 1 Sam. 10:24; 2 Sam. 16:16; 1 Kings 1:25, 39.) God had kept His covenant promise and put one of David's descendants on the throne of Judah!

Obedience (2 Kings 11:13-21; 2 Chron. 23:12-21)

God had protected the young king and had enabled Jehoiada and the officers to present him to the people, but the work wasn't over yet.

The execution of Athaliah (vv. 13-16; 23:12-15). The repeated shout "God save the king!" startled Athaliah and she hastened out of the palace to see what was happening. The first thing she discovered was that she was trapped. There were guards around the palace and between the palace and the temple courts, so there was no opportunity for her to escape or for her own soldiers to come to her rescue. She hurried to the temple court where she saw the young king standing by the pillar (1 Kings 7:21), protected by the captains. She also saw that the assembly was made up not only of priests, Levites and military personnel, but also "the people of the land," that is, the land-holding citizens whose work, wealth, and influence were important to the nation.

How paradoxical that she should shout "Treason! Treason!" when *she* was the real traitor. Joash was a descendant of David and had every right to the throne, while Athaliah had seized the throne and had no claim to it. Jehoiada ordered the five military captains to escort her out of the temple area and told the guards to slay anybody who followed her. Once they were back on the palace grounds, near the Horse Gate, they killed her with the sword.

The dedication of the people (v. 17; 23:16). Jehoiada had already given the holy covenant to the king (v. 12), but it was necessary that both the people and the king affirm their allegiance to one another and to the Lord. Israel was a theocracy and God was their King. The king ruled as God's chosen representative, and the people obeyed the king as they would obey the Lord, for the law of Israel was the law of the Lord. Israel was a covenant nation, for at Mount Sinai their ancestors had sworn allegiance to the Lord and His Word (Ex. 18–19). *No other nation on earth has this same covenant relationship to the Lord* (Ps. 147:19-20).

The elimination of Baal worship (vv. 18-21; 23:17). As Jehu had done in Samaria, so Jehoiada did in Jerusalem: he and the people destroyed the temple of Baal and killed the chief priest of Baal before the altar of Baal.[2] No doubt they also executed the other people who were leaders in Baal worship. They also destroyed the temple of Baal and the altar and images that it contained. Because of Athaliah and her compromising husband Jehoram and their son Ahaziah, the kingdom of Judah had been infected with idolatry for at least fifteen years, and now the infection was exposed and removed.

The restoration of the Davidic dynasty (11:19-21; 23:20-21). What a joyful crowd it was that escorted the king from the temple to the palace, where they placed him on the throne! Satan's attempt to end the Davidic line had failed, and the messianic promise was still in force. The people had done the will of God and obeyed His Word, and for the first time in many years, righteousness and peace reigned in the land.

The organization of the temple ministry (11:18b; 2 Chron. 23:18-19). We learn from 2 Kings 12 that the temple of the Lord had been grossly neglected and abused during the time that Athaliah was the power behind the throne. Jehoiada immediately took steps to remedy this situation by following David's orders (1 Chron. 23–26) and putting the proper priests and Levites into places of ministry. It was important that they offer the daily sacrifices to the Lord and sing praises to Him. It was also essential that the doors of the temple be guarded so that no unclean person might enter and defile the other worshipers. *Revival is simply obeying God's Word and doing what He commanded our fathers to do.* We don't need the novelties of the present; we need the realities of the past.

When God began to restore true worship in Jerusalem and Judah, He started with one dedicated couple—Jehoiada the high priest and his wife Jehosheba. They enlisted the nurse who cared for Joash, and God protected all four of them for six years. Then Jehoiada enlisted the five military captains, who in turn assembled their five hundred soldiers. The scattered priests, Levites, and people of the land came together as one to honor the Lord and obey His Word. Sin was purged, God's will was accomplished and the name of the Lord was glorified!

God could do it then, and He can do it today—but we must trust Him to have His way.

SEVEN

2 KINGS 12–13
[2 CHRONICLES 24]

Focusing on Faith

It's a well-known principle that what a person believes ulti-mately determines how a person behaves. Eve believed the Devil's lie that she wouldn't die; she ate the forbidden fruit, and she eventually died. With his eyes wide open, Adam believed he should imitate his wife, so he took the fruit and ate it; and he plunged the human race into sin and death (Gen. 3; Rom. 5:12-21; 1 Tim. 2:14). When we believe the truth, God works *for* us, but when we believe a lie, the Devil works *against* us. When our Lord was tempted by Satan, He countered Satan's lies with God's truth and said, "It is written" (Matt. 4:1-11). The three kings pre-sented in these chapters illustrate three different kinds of faith, none of which is the kind God's people should have today.

Joash—shallow faith (2 Kings 12:1-21)
In His parable about the sower (Matt. 13:1-9, 18-23), Jesus explained that, from a spiritual viewpoint, there are four kinds of hearts, and they respond to the seed of the Word in four differ-ent ways. When the hard-hearted hear the Word, the seed can't get in, so Satan snatches it away. Shallow-hearted people receive the Word but provide no room for it to take root, so the shoots

grow up but don't last. A plant can't grow and bear fruit if it doesn't have roots. Those with crowded hearts receive the seed but the shoots are smothered by the weeds that should have been pulled up. The person with the heart that bears fruit is honest, repentant, understands the Word and embraces it by faith. When it came to his own personal faith, King Joash had a shallow heart. Let's note the stages in Joash's spiritual experience.

Obeying (vv. 1-3; 2 Chron. 24:1-3). Joash was only seven years old when he ascended the throne of Judah (11:4), and he had a long reign of forty years. It's obvious that a child of seven can't rule a nation, so the high priest Jehoiada was his tutor and mentor. Joash seemed to be a willing student, and during all the years that Jehoiada instructed him, the king obeyed the Lord. When the king was ready for marriage, it was Jehoiada who picked out his two wives. Both David and Solomon had gotten into trouble because of too many unwise marriages, so the high priest limited Joash to two wives. It was important that Joash rebuild the family of David, for the house of David had almost been destroyed by Jehoram (2 Chron. 21:4), Jehu (2 Kings 10:12-14), Arab invaders (2 Chron. 22:1), and Queen Athaliah (2 Kings 11:1).

The only thing Joash and Jehoiada didn't do was remove the high places in Judah, the local shrines where the people worshiped the Lord. They were supposed to go to the temple to worship (Deut. 12), but during the dark days of Athaliah's reign, the temple had been ignored and even allowed to decay. However, Jehoiada and King Joash would lead the people in repairing the temple so that they had a fine place for worshiping the Lord. The godly people in Judah must have rejoiced that an obedient descendant of David was on the throne. What they didn't know was that Joash's faith was shallow, and that he obeyed God only to please Jehoiada. Joash was an excellent follower but not a good leader. When Jehoiada died, Joash went his own way and disobeyed the Lord.

Struggling (vv. 4-16; 2 Chron. 24:4-14). It was clear to the people of Judah that godly Jehoiada was the power behind the throne, and this probably gave them a feeling of security. But as the king matured in age and experience, he must have been frustrated by this arrangement. It's a normal thing for young people to want the freedom to be themselves and make their own decisions, and this desire must have been intensified in Joash's life because of the authority he possessed. But with Jehoiada running things, Joash could say with King David, "And I am weak today, though anointed king" (2 Sam. 3:39, NKJV).

It isn't easy to mentor a young king and know just when to loosen and lengthen the restraining cords. Parents know this from raising their children to adulthood. Perhaps Jehoiada was taking charge too much and not gradually handing responsibility over to Joash. On the other hand, perhaps Jehoiada held the reins longer because he saw some weaknesses in the king's character and wanted to give him time to correct them. Maybe it was just a "generational problem." Whatever the cause, the king decided it was time to be set free from the rule of the Jewish priesthood and to begin to assert his authority. He chose the repairing of the temple as his focal point for freedom.

No doubt Joash and Jehoiada had discussed the need for repairing the temple, but for some reason, the high priest wasn't enthusiastic enough to get things started. Old age may have been a factor. We don't know how old Joash was when Jehoiada issued the order to have the temple offerings diverted into the building project (vv. 4-5). This would include money from the census (Ex. 30:11-16; Num. 2:32), money from personal vows (Lev. 22:18-23; 27:1ff), and money from the trespass offerings (v. 17; Lev. 5:14-6:7). But the plan didn't work, probably because the priests depended on these sources of income for the funds they needed to maintain the temple ministry and to meet their own needs. As far as the census was concerned, the priests and Levites may have hesitated because they remembered that David's census had brought judgment to the land (1 Chron. 22).

The text doesn't tell us how long Joash waited for Jehoiada to act, but when he was thirty years old and had reigned for twenty-three years, the king decided to act on his own. He called in Jehoiada and cautiously rebuked the priests for not doing the job.

He also told the high priest that the throne would now direct the building program. The priests could keep the money that was rightfully theirs according the Mosaic Law, because the new approach to financing the project would be freewill offerings from the people. Jehoiada informed the priests and Levites, who must have rejoiced that their income wouldn't be diverted and that they no longer had to get involved in repairing the temple. Having been involved in church building programs, I can sympathize with them!

The arrangement was simple, and it worked. Jehoiada prepared a large offering box, placed it in the temple by an entrance near the altar, and encouraged the people to bring their offerings for the repair of the temple. Of course, there were temple guards that kept their eye on the box. When the people found out that the project was now under royal supervision and in the hands of the laity, this encouraged them to give even more. They knew that every gift they brought and placed in the box would go directly into the building project and not be diverted into other ministries, so they gave generously. King Josiah followed a similar plan when he repaired the temple nearly two hundred years later (2 Kings 22:1-7).

However, Joash didn't ignore the priesthood in this project, for the counting and distributing of the money was handled jointly by representatives of the king and the high priest (v. 10). Without realizing it, Joash was following Paul's principle of involving the people and making sure everything was kept open and aboveboard (2 Cor. 8:16-24). The workers were so honest and faithful that nobody kept records of the income and expenditures, a fact that may have upset the royal auditors. The only project they didn't include was replacing the gold and silver utensils that had been stolen from the temple (2 Chron. 24:7), but enough money was left over to take care of that need (2 Chron. 24:14).

Believers today know that the Lord doesn't live in church buildings or in any other kind of building (John 4:23-24; Acts 7:48-50; 17:24), but this doesn't mean that it's wrong to dedicate structures to His service and glory. The early churches didn't have their own buildings but met in homes and in accessible public places such as the temple in Jerusalem. It wasn't until the fourth century that the law permitted them to construct and meet in their own buildings. Some of the saints today oppose church buildings and say they're a waste of God's money, while others almost worship their buildings and get their priorities confused. Campbell Morgan clarifies the issue with this warning:

> Whereas the house of God today is no longer material but spiritual, the material is still a very real symbol of the spiritual. When the Church of God in any place in any locality is careless about the material place of assembly, the place of its worship and its work, it is a sign and evidence that its life is at a low ebb.[1]

I recall preaching one Sunday evening to a congregation that met in a church building that was in such disrepair that it couldn't help but embarrass the members and the visitors they brought. It was doubtful that any of the members lived in houses in that condition (Hag. 1:1-6). I asked one of the church leaders why they didn't fix things up, and he replied somewhat sarcastically, "Oh, most of our budget has to go to foreign missions. And do you know what the missionaries do with the money we send them? They fix their buildings!" It wasn't a matter of either home or foreign but of balance. As Dr. Oswald J. Smith used to say, "The light that shines the farthest will shine the brightest at home." The executive director of a foreign mission ministry told me, "It took me ten years to learn that Acts 1:8 didn't use the word *or* but the word *and*. The Lord doesn't tear things down at home in order to build things up overseas." Blessed are the balanced!

Forsaking (vv. 17-18; 2 Chron. 24:15-22). Jehoiada died at the advanced age of one hundred and thirty. He was so beloved by the people that he was buried with the kings (2 Chron. 24:15-16). But when Jehoiada passed off the scene, King Joash showed his true colors and abandoned the faith. His apostasy wasn't the fault of Jehoiada, for the high priest had faithfully taught Joash the Scriptures. The problem was Joash's shallow faith and his desire to please the leaders of the land, "the officials of Judah" who visited Joash and asked him to be more lenient in matters of religion (24:17-18). He relented, and once again idolatry moved into Judah and Jerusalem.

Joash's apostasy was a sin of willful rebellion against God, for the king knew what the Law of Moses taught about idolatry. But it was also a sin of ingratitude for all that Jehoiada had done for him. *Jehoiada and his wife had saved the king's life!* The high priest had taught him the truth of God's Word and had stood at Joash's side as he learned how to govern the people. But the king had never taken the truth into his heart and allowed it to take root. The soil of his heart was shallow and he had obeyed God's law only because his mentor was watching. He even took wealth from the very temple he had repaired and gave it to a pagan king for ransom!

Joash is a warning to us today. It isn't enough simply to know God's truth; we must obey His truth "from the heart" (Eph. 6:6). Truth in the mind can lead to obedience, but truth in the heart and obedience from the heart will produce godly character. God's Word and God's will must be internalized—received into the heart (Ps. 119:9-11)—or we can never develop consistent Christian character. Until duty and discipline become delight, we are only reluctant servants who obey God because we have to, not because we want to. Jehoiada was a "religious prop" on which the king leaned. When the prop was removed, the king fell.

During more than fifty years of ministry, I have occasionally witnessed the "Joash tragedy." A godly wife dies and the widower soon drops out of church and starts to live a worldly life. Sons or daughters go off to college and gradually leave the faith because father and mother aren't there to counsel and warn them. I've known some high-profile Christian leaders who "used" their children in their ministries, but when the children were on their own, they turned their backs on their parents and the Lord.

A good beginning is no guarantee of a good ending. King Josiah had every encouragement to become a godly man, but he didn't take advantage of his opportunities by taking God's truth into his heart. When the Lord sent prophets to warn him, he refused to listen. He even plotted with his leaders to have Zechariah, the son of Jehoiada, stoned to death because he rebuked the king for his sins.[2] Imagine murdering the son of the very people who saved your life!

Suffering (vv. 19-21; 2 Chron. 24:23-27). When the king of Judah became an idolater and a murderer, the Lord began to discipline him. First He brought the prophets to warn Joash, but he wouldn't listen. Then He brought Judah's long-time enemy Syria against Judah,[3] and Joash was severely wounded in the battle. He finally robbed the temple and bribed Hazael not to attack Jerusalem. However, Joash didn't recover from his wounds, for two of his officials murdered him because he had ordered the death of Zechariah, son of Jehoiada.[4] Second Chronicles 24:26 informs us that the two assassins were sons of non-Jewish women, one from Moab and the other from Ammon. The Moabites and the Ammonites were the descendants of Abraham's nephew Lot who had an incestuous relationship with his two daughters (Gen. 19:30-38). The people buried Joash in Jerusalem but not in the sepulcher of the kings where Jehoiada the high priest was buried (2 Chron. 24:25, 16).

The boy king, who made such a good beginning, had a bad ending, and it was because he forsook the way of the Lord. We wonder if the Prophet Ezekiel was thinking about Joash when he wrote Ezekiel 18:24-32.

Jehoahaz—crisis faith (2 Kings 13:1-9)

Now the focus moves from Judah to Israel and the reign of Jehu's son Jehoahaz. It's no surprise that he chose Jeroboam as his model, because his father had done the same thing (10:29). Jehoahaz would rather worship the golden calves than the living God, but when he found himself in trouble, he turned to the Lord for help.

The people of Israel shouldn't have been surprised when the Lord brought the Syrians against them, because the people knew the terms of the covenant God had made with them before they entered the land of Canaan. If they obeyed Him, He would give them victory over their enemies, but if they disobeyed, He would cause them to fall before their enemies (Lev. 26:17, 25, 33, 36-39; Deut. 28:25-26, 49-52). People still believe Satan's lie, "You will not surely die" (Gen. 3:4, NKJV). "Do whatever you enjoy," says the Enemy, "because there are no serious consequences to sin." But whether to chasten or to bless, God is always true to His Word.

The situation became so painfully desperate that Jehoahaz cried out to God for help, just the way Israel had done during the period of the judges (Jud. 2:10-23). God in His mercy heard and answered the king's prayer and promised to send a deliverer, but only after Jehoahaz was off the scene (v. 22). Hazael died and his son and successor Ben-Hadad was a weaker ruler, so it was possible for someone to break the iron grip Syria had on Israel. Historians aren't agreed as to who this deliverer was. Some point to the Assyrians who began to attack Syria in the days of Ben-Hadad and weaken his power. Others feel the deliverance came through one or both of Jehoahaz's successors, Jehoash (v. 25) and Jeroboam II (14:25-27). The statement "Israel dwelt in their tents" (v. 5) means "they lived in peace and didn't have to seek refuge in the walled cities."

Did the promised blessing of God change the king? Apparently not, for he didn't remove the idols from the land (v. 6; 1 Kings 16:33) nor did he encourage the people to return to the Lord. Crisis faith is rarely deep or lasting. Once people see hope of deliverance and their pain eases up, they forget the Lord and return to their old ways until the next crisis. The Syrians left Jehoahaz with a mock army that was more of an embarrassment than it was an encouragement. Yet God had promised that if His people trusted Him and obeyed His Word, their enemies would flee before them (Deut. 28:7; 32:30; Lev. 26:8).

But crisis faith is undependable. How many times I've heard

hospital patients say, "Pastor, if God heals me and gets me out of here, I'll be the best Christian you ever met." God did heal them and allow them to go home, but I never met them again in church. Yes, there are such things as "foxhole conversions" and "deathbed conversions," and we don't want to discourage anyone from turning to God in the hour of crisis. The British historian William Camden wrote, "Betwixt the stirrup and the ground / Mercy I asked, mercy I found."

But how many times can we call on the Lord when we're in trouble and then ignore Him when we're safe? People who depend on crisis faith need to heed the warnings of Proverbs 1:24-33 and Isaiah 55:6-7, and they shouldn't assume that because God heard and helped them, they're automatically going to heaven.

Jehoash—ignorant faith (2 Kings 13:10-25)

For some reason, the death of Jehoash is mentioned twice, once before the historian records his life (vv. 12-13) and again at the end of the story (14:15-16). His great defeat of Amaziah, king of Judah, is also mentioned before it's described (14:8-14; 2 Chron. 25). But the most important thing about Jehoash was that he had sense enough to visit the Prophet Elisha and seek some blessing from him. Consider five facts about Jehoash.

He followed the wrong examples (vv. 10-13). Like his father, he modeled himself after Jeroboam I, the first king of Israel. This meant he visited the golden calves and bowed down to idols. And, like his father, he turned to the Lord only when he was in trouble and time was running out. The Syrians were still in control and the Prophet Elisha was about to die.

He made a wise decision (v. 14). We haven't heard from or about Elisha since 9:1, when he sent one of the sons of the prophets to anoint Jehu to be king of Israel. This means over forty years of silence as far as the record is concerned, yet Elisha was at work in the land and the Lord was with him. Now he was an old man and about to die, and the king of Israel went to see him. Let's at least give Jehoash credit for visiting the prophet and seeking his help. Was it Elisha who told Jehoahaz that God would send a deliverer (vv. 4-5)? Was his son Jehoash that deliverer? Only Elisha knew God's plan and the king was wise enough to visit him.

It's too bad spiritual leaders aren't appreciated during their lifetime but are greatly lauded after they die. The Pharisees were better at building tombs for the dead than they were at showing thanks to the living (Matt. 23:29-32). Faithful servants of God never "retire" even though they may leave their lifelong vocation and step back from public ministry. Even from his deathbed, Elisha was serving the Lord and his people. As long as God gives us strength and sanity, we should serve Him the best we can in whatever ways He opens for us. How grateful I am for "senior servants" who have counseled and encouraged me, and the memories of their lives and ministries are still a blessing to me (Heb. 13:7-8, NIV).

The king showed respect for the prophet and even addressed him with the same words Elisha used for Elijah when Elijah was taken to heaven (2:12). Elisha was like a father to the nation and was more valuable than all their armies! Elisha knew that Jehoash was in trouble because of the Syrians and graciously used his failing strength to help the king. Yes, Jehoash was a compromising king who disobeyed God, but Jehovah is "the Lord, the Lord God, merciful and gracious, longsuffering, and abounding in goodness and truth" (Ex. 34:6, NKJV). He had promised deliverance for His people and He would keep His promise. However, Elisha gave Jehoash God's promise of victory but did it in a way that required the king to exercise intelligent faith.

He made a great mistake (vv. 15-19). King Jehoash was not a man of faith, but he could follow directions. However, he lacked the spiritual discernment and insight that people have who live in the Word and walk by faith. When the prophet put his hands on the king's hands, it obviously symbolized a conveying of power from God. When Elisha commanded him to shoot an arrow toward the area where the Syrians were in control, it clearly spoke of victory over the enemy (Deut. 32:42; Ps. 120:4). This much the king could have understood because Elisha gave him a clear promise of victory.

But when Elisha told him to take the remaining arrows and strike the ground with them, he didn't have the spiritual understanding he needed to make the most of it. Had he been a faithful worshiper of the living God, he would have seen the truth; but he was blind like the dead idols he worshiped (Ps. 115:3-8). Shooting one arrow guaranteed victory, but the number of times he smote the ground determined how many victories God would give him. Because Jehoash had ignorant faith, he limited himself to only three victories over the Syrians.

As sick as he was, the Prophet Elisha expressed righteous anger over the king's ignorance and unbelief. What an opportunity Jehoash missed for utterly destroying his enemies! "According to your faith let it be to you" (Matt. 9:29, NKJV). It isn't enough for us simply to *know* God's will and obey it, as important as that is, but we should also *understand* God's will and God's ways (Eph. 5:17; Ps. 103:7). The commandments and acts of God reveal to us the character of God if our spiritual eyes are open (Eph. 1:17-20). This is how we understand the ways of God and how better to serve Him, and this is how the Lord increases our faith.

He received a great encouragement (vv. 20-21). When Elisha died, the king may have wondered if his promises died with him. To encourage the king, the Lord graciously performed a miracle after Elisha died. The Jews didn't embalm corpses as did the Egyptians. They merely washed the body and wrapped it in clean cloths along with spices. One day, when the arrival of Moabite raiders interrupted a committal service of a man recently deceased, the mourners quickly put the body into Elisha's tomb and fled. But God used that occasion to give the man life! Surely this miracle was talked about among the people and the king may have heard the account from the lips of the men who saw it. This miracle told him that, though the prophet was dead, Jehovah was still the living God and the God of power. His promises would not fail.

The Prophet Elijah never died but was caught up into heaven (2:11-12), but the Prophet Elisha died and was buried. However,

Elisha performed a miracle even after he was dead. God has different plans for each of His servants and it's not our business to compare one with the other or to question what He does (John 21:19-23).

He won the three victories (vv. 22-25). The Syrians were determined to destroy Israel and make it a part of their empire, but the Lord had other plans. His covenant with the patriarchs (Gen. 12:1-3) and His grace toward their descendants moved Him to look upon Israel's affliction and rescue them from their enemies. It was only when the people sinned so flagrantly that they blasphemed the name of the Lord and defiled His land that God permitted both Israel and Judah to be defeated and taken into bondage. In 722, Assyria conquered the northern kingdom of Israel, and in 586, Jerusalem fell to the Babylonians. The people of Judah returned to their land after the seventy years of captivity expired, but the people of Israel were assimilated into the Assyrian empire.

King Jehoash won three great victories against the Syrians, and this was sufficient to enable him to recover towns that Hazael and Ben-Hadad had taken from Israel, and then King Jeroboam II recovered the rest of the land. The Lord enabled Jehoash to increase his military power (v. 7) and overcome the Syrians led by Ben-Hadad III. God's promise came true and God's people were spared. During the reigns of Jehoash and Jeroboam II, the kingdom of Israel reached its zenith and there was prosperity in the land. However, with all its achievements and wealth, it was still a land filled with idolatry and much sin. During the reign of Jeroboam II, the Prophets Hosea and Amos ministered to the people of Israel. When you read their books, you see the true conditions of the land.

EIGHT

2 KINGS 14–15
[2 CHRONICLES 25–27]

Nine Kings—Five Assassinations

"Political history is far too criminal and pathological to be a fit subject of study for the young," wrote poet W. H. Auden. Edward Gibbon, author of *The Decline and Fall of the Roman Empire*, defined history as "little more than the register of the crimes, follies, and misfortunes of mankind."[1]

The history recorded in these five chapters seems to agree with Auden and Gibbon, for it reeks of selfish intrigue, bloodshed, moral decay, and repeated rebellion against the law of the Lord. Ancient Israel wasn't much different from society today. Not one king of Israel encouraged his people to repent and seek the Lord; and in Judah, Amaziah and Uzziah both committed acts of arrogant ambition that brought judgment from God. When Jeroboam II became king of Israel in 782 B.C., little did the people realize that in sixty years, the kingdom would be no more. As we look at these nine rulers, we can gain some practical insights into the will and ways of God as well as the terrible wages of sin.

Amaziah, a presumptuous king (2 Kings 14:1-20; 2 Chron. 25)
Amaziah was the ninth king of Judah[2] and the son of Joash (Jehoash), the "boy king," who in his later years turned away

from the Lord, killed God's prophet, and was himself assassinated (2 Chron. 24:15-26). Amaziah made an excellent beginning, but he later abandoned the Lord and was also assassinated (14:17-20).[3] He saw to it that the men were executed who had killed his father, and he obeyed Deuteronomy 24:16 by judging only the offenders and not their families.[4] Had he continued to obey God's Word, his life and reign would have been much different. Consider some of his sins.

Unbelief (14:7; 25:5-13). Amaziah decided to attack Edom and regain territory that had been lost (8:20-22). The venture was a good one, but the way he went about it was definitely wrong. He took a census and found he had 300,000 men, but instead of trusting the Lord to use these men, he hired 100,000 mercenaries from Israel to increase his forces. His faith was in numbers and not in the Lord (Ps. 20:7), but even worse, the soldiers he hired came from apostate Israel where the people worshiped the golden calves. God sent a prophet to rebuke the king and warn him that the Lord was not with the kingdom of Israel, so the hired soldiers would only bring defeat. "But if you go, be gone! Be strong in battle! Even so, God shall make you fall before the enemy; for God has power to help and to overthrow" (25:8, NKJV). The prophet was a bit sarcastic, but he made his point.

One of the recurring themes in Israel's history is their sin of forming alliances with the ungodly because they didn't have faith in the Lord. Solomon married heathen wives and by this entered into treaties with his neighbors, but his wives influenced him to worship idols (1 Kings 11). King Ahab married Jezebel, a Phoenician princess and a worshiper of Baal (1 Kings 16:30-33), and this brought Baal worship into the kingdom. King Jehoshaphat allied with Ahab to fight the Syrians and was almost killed. Jehoshaphat also entered into a business partnership with King Ahaziah, but the Lord broke it up by destroying Jehoshaphat's fleet. "Do not be unequally yoked together with unbelievers" (2 Cor. 6:14, NKJV) is an admonition that needs to be heard and heeded by the church today. It's not by imitating the world and uniting with the world, but by being different from the world that we manifest the power and grace of God and accomplish His will.

According to 2 Chron. 25:2, Amaziah was not wholehearted in his relationship to the Lord (see NIV), and this revealed itself in the way he argued with the prophet about the will of God (25:9). The king was unwilling to send the mercenaries home because it would have meant forfeiting the one hundred talents of silver he had paid to the king of Israel. This amounted to nearly four tons of silver. Amaziah was "counting the cost" and adjusting his priorities, hoping he could change God's mind. The prophet wisely replied that God could give him much more if he would only trust Him and obey His will (Matt. 6:33).

If we would seek the Lord's will *before* we rush into disobedience, we would avoid a great deal of trouble; but even after we change our minds and decide to obey the Lord, often there are still painful consequences to endure. The soldiers returned to Israel very angry because of the way they had been treated. Why were they angry? For one thing, they lost an opportunity to profit from the spoils of battle. Furthermore, who was the king of Judah to say that God thought more highly of Judah's soldiers than He did the army of Samaria? What an embarrassment for these brave mercenaries to be sent home empty-handed, having never fought the battle! How could they explain to the king and their friends back home that the army had been declared unclean and rejected? Their solution was to give vent to their anger by attacking some of the border cities in northern Judah. They killed three thousand people and took the spoils as their compensation (25:13).[5]

Because he finally obeyed the Lord, Amaziah's army defeated the Edomites. They killed ten thousand men in the Valley of Salt, where David had won a great victory (1 Chron. 18:12). Then they destroyed ten thousand prisoners of war by casting them down from the heights of the city of Sela (Petra) that was cut right out of the mountain (Obad. 1-4). So elated was Amaziah with his achievement that he renamed the city "Joktheel," which means "God destroys" (14:7).

Idolatry (25:14-16). The saintly Scottish minister Andrew Bonar said, "Let us be as watchful after the victory as before the battle," an admonition that King Amaziah desperately needed to hear and heed. The Lord Jehovah had given His servant an outstanding victory over a strong enemy in a difficult place, *and yet Amaziah took back to Judah the gods of the defeated enemy* (2 Chron. 25:14-16)! Surely the king of Judah didn't think that by taking these idols he would paralyze the Edomites and prevent future wars! Every Jew was taught that the Lord Jehovah was one God and the only true and living God, and therefore the gods of the nations were nothing (Deut. 6:4-5; Ps. 115). Worshiping idols was a direct violation of the Law of Moses (Ex. 20:1-6), and worshiping the gods of a defeated enemy was simply unreasonable. After all, what did those gods accomplish for the Edomites? Yet Amaziah began to worship the gods of Edom, offer them sacrifices, and consult them.

When the Lord sent His messenger to the king to warn him, Amaziah interrupted the prophet and threatened to kill him if he continued to speak. But the prophet had one last word: God would destroy the king for his sin. In fact, God would permit the king to destroy himself! The greatest judgment God can send to people is to let them have their own way.

Pride (14:8-14; 25:17-24). Amaziah defeated the Edomites because he obeyed the Lord, but then the Edomites defeated Amaziah when he took their gods home with him. Inflated by his great success and unconcerned about his great sin, Amaziah looked for other worlds to conquer and decided to challenge Joash (Jehoash), king of Israel. He not only ignored the warning of the prophet God sent, but he forgot the words of his ancestor Solomon, "Before destruction the heart of man is haughty, and before honor is humility" (Prov. 18:12, NKJV). Even King Jehoash warned him that his pride would ruin him (14:10), but Amaziah was bent on defeating Israel and becoming the ruler of a united kingdom.

Jehoash's reply (14:9; 25:18) reminds us of the parable Jotham spoke (Jud. 9:7-20), and both of them deal with pride and judgment. Amaziah's problem was pride: he saw himself as a strong cedar, when in reality he was only a weak thistle that could be crushed by a passing wild beast. The truly humble person sees things as God sees them and doesn't live on illusions. Pride blinds the mind, distorts the vision and so inflates the ego that the person can't tell truth from fiction.

Rejecting a second warning from the Lord, Amaziah invaded Israel where his army was soundly defeated. He was taken captive fifteen miles from Jerusalem and went from the palace to the prison. The army of Israel invaded Judah and destroyed six hundred feet of the wall of Jerusalem, leaving the city vulnerable to future attacks. They also took treasures from the palace and from the temple of the Lord, and they even took some of the leaders as hostages. King Amaziah was in exile in Samaria for fifteen years (14:17) and then returned to Jerusalem briefly as coregent with his son (14:21; 26:1, 3). But his idolatry disturbed some of the leaders and they formed a conspiracy to assassinate him. He fled to Lachish where he was captured and killed (14:18-20; 25:27).

Amaziah is a tragic figure in Jewish history. He was presented with great opportunities and experienced great help from the Lord, but he was a double-minded man who didn't wholeheartedly serve the Lord. He had his own agenda and didn't take time to seek the mind of the Lord. "Pride goes before destruction, and a haughty spirit before a fall" (Prov. 16:18, NKJV).

Jeroboam, a prosperous king (14:23-29)
The record now turns from Judah to Israel and to Jeroboam II who had the longest reign of any of Israel's kings, forty-one years. He was not a good king when it came to spiritual matters, but he brought prosperity to the nation and delivered it from its enemies. Even back in those ancient days, the average citizen didn't care about the character of the nation's leaders so long as the people had food on their tables, money in their purses, and no fear of being invaded by their enemies.

Thanks to Assyria's victories over Syria, both Israel and Judah were finally relieved of the bondage of that persistent enemy and both had opportunity to use their wealth and manpower for building instead of battling. Israel was able to drive the Syrians out of the border outposts and Jeroboam also recovered the territory that had been lost to Syria. The kingdom of Israel reached the dimensions achieved in the days of Solomon (vv. 25 and 28; 1 Kings 8:65). The Lord permitted these victories, not because the people or their king deserved them, but because He had pity on His people who were suffering under the rule of Syria (14:26; see Ex. 2:23-25).

But the prosperity of Israel was only a veneer that covered sins and crimes that were an abomination in the sight of the Lord. The Prophets Amos (1:1) and Hosea (1:1) ministered during Jeroboam's reign and warned that judgment was coming. Judgment did come in 722 B.C., when the Assyrians invaded Israel, deported many of the Jewish people and imported Gentiles from other conquered nations to mix with the Israelites. This policy eventually produced a mixed race, part Jew and part Gentile, as well as a hybrid religion with its own temple and priesthood on Mount Gerizim (John 4:20-22). After the Babylonian captivity, the orthodox Jews who returned to Judah would have nothing to do with the Samaritans (Ezra 4:1-4; Neh. 2:19-20; see John 4:9).

What were the sins of this prosperous kingdom? For one thing, the rich were getting richer at the expense of the poor, who were exploited and abused. The wealthy landowners barely cared for their slaves, and the courts disobeyed the law and decided cases in favor of the rich and not in fairness to the poor. In the midst of this corruption, the leaders practiced their "religion," attended services, and brought their sacrifices (Amos 2:1-8; 4:1-5). While the wealthy men and their wives lived in luxury, the poor were downtrodden and robbed of their civil rights (Amos 6:1-7; Hos. 12:8). The "religious" crowd longed for "the day of the Lord" to come, thinking that this momentous event would bring even greater glory to Israel (Amos 5:18-27). The people didn't realize that "the day of the Lord" actually meant divine judgment on the nation, for God's judgment begins with His own

NINE KINGS — FIVE ASSASSINATIONS

people (1 Peter 4:17). Israel was given to idolatry, which led to moral decay and worldly corruption (Hos. 6:4; 7:8; 9:9; 11:7; 13:2).[6] Jeroboam II ruled from 793 to 753, and in 722 B.C. the Assyrians invaded Israel and brought to an end the nation of Israel.

British poet and playwright Oliver Goldsmith said it perfectly in his poem *The Deserted Village*:

> Ill fares the land, to hast'ning ills a prey,
> Where wealth accumulates, and men decay . . .

Uzziah (Azariah), an illustrious king (2 Kings 15:1-7; 2 Chron. 26)
His given name was Azariah, which means "Jehovah has helped," but when he became king of Judah at age sixteen, he took the "throne name" Uzziah, which means "Jehovah is strength." The people made him king when his father Azariah was taken to Samaria after his foolish war against Jehoash, king of Israel (2 Kings 14:13).

During his father's fifteen years of captivity in Samaria, Uzziah ruled Judah and sought to do the will of God. After his father's death, Uzziah continued on the throne until he foolishly attempted to become a priest and God judged him by making him a leper. At that time, his son Jotham became coregent with his father. The record declares that Uzziah was king of Judah fifty-two years (2 Chron. 26:3), including his coregencies with his father Azariah (fifteen years) and also with his son Jotham (possibly ten years).

From the very beginning of his reign, Uzziah showed himself to be a faithful worshiper of Jehovah, even though he didn't try to eliminate the "high places," the hill shrines where the Jewish people worshiped. They were supposed to go to the temple with their gifts and sacrifices for the Lord, but it was more convenient to visit a local shrine. Some of the high places were still devoted to pagan deities, such as Baal (2 Chron. 27:2), and it wasn't until the reigns of Hezekiah and Josiah that the high places were removed (2 Chron. 31:1; 2 Kings 23).

Uzziah's accomplishments (2 Kings 14:22; 2 Chron. 26:2, 6-15). He was very successful in his military exploits. He recovered from Edom the city of Elath, although later it was lost to Syria and Israel (2 Kings 16:5-6; 2 Chron. 28:17). Their possessing Elath gave Judah access to the sea, and this helped in their trade with other nations. Uzziah had Zechariah as his counselor and sought to know and please the Lord. "As long as he sought the Lord, God made him to prosper" (26:5).

God prospered his armies and helped them to conquer the Philistines, the Arabians, and the Ammonites. After defeating the Philistines, he destroyed the walls of their key cities. This victory gave him additional access to the sea. To keep control over this newly acquired territory, Uzziah built cities in Philistia and settled them with Jewish soldiers and officers. After conquering the Ammonites, Uzziah's fame increased even more. But these victories on foreign soil didn't deter him from strengthening things at home. He built towers on the walls of Jerusalem and repaired the damage that was done by the army of Israel (2 Kings 14:13). He had a well-trained army and provided them with the weapons and armor they needed,[7] and he also encouraged the building of "war machines" that shot arrows and threw stones (26:11-15).

But Uzziah wasn't just a gifted soldier and a careful builder; he was also a farmer at heart. He sought to develop the land by building cisterns and putting the people to work with the flocks and herds as well as the fields and vineyards. He built towers in the fields where the guards could watch for invaders and protect the people. "Those who labor in the earth are the chosen people of God," wrote Thomas Jefferson in his *Notes on the State of Virginia*. Though a soldier, a builder, and a monarch, Uzziah was a man of the soil. He would have agreed with Booker T. Washington who said, "[T]here is as much dignity in tilling a field as in writing a poem."

Uzziah's arrogance (15:5; 26:16-21). Unfortunately, Uzziah imitated his father and allowed his accomplishments to swell his head. Amaziah wanted to be known as a great general, but

Uzziah wanted to serve as both king and priest. In the Old Testament economy, the Lord separated the kings and priests, and while a priest could become a prophet (Ezekiel, Zechariah, John the Baptist), no prophet or king could become a priest. Only in Jesus Christ do we find the offices of prophet, priest, and king combined, and His priesthood is "after the order of Melchizedek" (Ps. 110:4; Gen. 14:18-20; Heb. 5–7). For Uzziah to covet the priesthood was ignorance, for he knew the Law of Moses; and for him to try to seize it by force was arrogance, for he knew what happened to others who had attempted to claim what wasn't rightfully theirs. (See Lev. 10; Num. 12, 16.)

"But when he became strong, his heart was so proud that he acted corruptly" (26:16, NASB). There's no question that Uzziah was an illustrious king whose name was known far and wide (26:15), but what the Lord did for him should have produced humility and not pride. Uzziah should have said with David, "Who am I, O Lord God? And what is my house that You have brought me thus far?" (2 Sam. 7:18, NKJV). Instead, he convinced himself that he deserved to be a priest as well as a king. He knew that the high priest burned the holy incense on the golden altar each morning and evening (Ex. 30:7-8), so he procured a censer and went into the temple precincts where only the priests were allowed to go (Num. 16:40; 18:7).

Azariah the high priest, along with eighty other priests, stood in his way and refused to allow him passage. It took a great deal of courage for them to oppose such a popular king, but their first allegiance was to the Lord. They could have compromised and perhaps won favors from the king, but they had but one desire, and that was to obey and glorify the Lord. The king became angry, refused to retreat, and raged at the priests for their interference. The Hebrew word translated "angry" in 26:19 implies "raging like a storm."

Had the king immediately left the temple and sincerely repented of his sins, the Lord would have forgiven him, but Uzziah stood his ground and insisted on his way. It was then that the Lord intervened and put the leprosy on his forehead where the priests could clearly see it. They knew that lepers belonged outside the camp, not inside the temple (Lev. 13:45-46), and they hurriedly forced the king out of the holy precincts. King Uzziah couldn't see the leprosy on his forehead, so perhaps it began to appear on other parts of his body so that he knew for certain that he was infected. The law demanded that those who intruded into the holy temple were to be put to death (Num. 18:7), but God graciously spared the king's life and gave him leprosy, a "living death."

Being a leper, the king couldn't appear in public or even live in the palace. He was quarantined in an isolated house while his son Jotham ruled the land as coregent. When Uzziah died, he was buried in the royal cemetery, but apparently not in the tombs of the kings. He had a wonderful beginning but a tragic ending, and this is a warning to us that we be on guard and pray that the Lord will help us to end well. A good beginning is no guarantee of a successful ending, and the sin of unholy ambition has ruined more than one servant of the Lord. Uzziah the soldier was defeated by his pride; Uzziah the builder destroyed his own ministry and testimony; and Uzziah the farmer reaped the painful harvest of what he had sown. He is a warning to all who nurture unholy ambitions to intrude into that which God hasn't appointed for them. (See Ps. 131.)

Five notorious kings (2 Kings 15:8-31)
From Jeroboam I, the first king of Israel, to Hoshea, the last king of Israel, not one king is called "good." However, the kingdom of Judah didn't fare much better, for out of twenty kings who ruled after the kingdom divided, only eight of them could be called "good."[8] In this section of 2 Kings, we meet with five kings of Israel who were notorious for their godless character and evil deeds. Four of them were assassinated! Shallum reigned only one month, Zechariah six months, and Pekahiah for two years. Menahem, the cruelest of them all, reigned for ten years, and Pekah for twenty years. As the Northern Kingdom stumbled toward destruction, their rulers hastened the coming of the judg-

NINE KINGS—FIVE ASSASSINATIONS

ment of God. God often gives a nation just exactly the leaders it deserves.

Zechariah (vv. 8-12). Twenty-nine men in Scripture are named Zechariah; this one was the son of Jeroboam II, the last great king of the northern kingdom of Israel. Zechariah didn't have the political skills of his father and he chose to imitate the sins of his namesake, Jeroboam I. Zechariah was the great-great-grandson of Jehu and therefore the last of that dynasty. God promised Jehu that his descendants would occupy the throne of Israel for four generations (2 Kings 10:30), and that promise was fulfilled. Zechariah was a king, not because of his sanctity, ability, or popularity, but because he was providentially born into the royal family. Only two major facts are recorded about him: he did evil in the sight of the Lord, and he was assassinated publicly by Shallum, who then took the throne. Zechariah reigned only six months, and his death ended Jehu's dynasty.

Shallum (vv. 13-15). We know very little about this man. He organized a conspiracy and murdered Zechariah; he reigned as king of Israel for one short month; and he was the victim of a conspiracy that led to his own death. "Whoever digs a pit will fall into it, and he who rolls a stone will have it roll back on him" (Prov. 26:27, NKJV). Shallum was killed by Menahem, one of his own officers who was military commander at Tirzah, the early capital of Samaria (1 Kings 14:17; 15:21, 33). If Shallum had any descendants, they probably didn't admit it. What was there about Shallum to be proud of?

Menahem (vv. 6-22). Since he was a man feared by the people and had the army under his control, Menahem was able to rule for ten years and die a natural death. Because the people of Tiphsah (a city we can't identify) wouldn't accept his kingship, he broke his way into the city and killed his enemies. He was a brutal man who followed the Syrian custom of ripping up pregnant women (v. 16; see 8:12), something that Hosea the Prophet warned would happen (Hos. 13:16). When the Assyrians invaded the land, Menahem taxed all the wealthy citizens over a pound of silver and gave Pul (Tiglath-Pileser) thirty-seven tons of silver as tribute. The Assyrians left, but they came back twenty years later and took over the entire land. King David would have trusted God, fought the Assyrians, and defeated them; but Menahem's policy was to compromise and conciliate.

Pekahiah (vv. 23-26). Menahem's son inherited the throne but ruled for only two years. His father had been a military commander and had assassinated King Shallum, and Pekahiah was killed in his own palace by Pekah, a military commander, who then became king. The fact that Pekah was assisted by fifty men from Gilead suggests that he was in charge of the military forces east of the Jordan River.[9] It's likely that Pekahiah and Pekah disagreed about the right policy Israel should follow regarding Assyria. Pekahiah, like his father Menahem, sought to appease the Assyrians and give them what they wanted, while Pekah, a military man, took a hard line against Assyria and favored Syria.

Pekah (vv. 27-31). Thanks to the protection of his army, Pekah was able to reign twenty years. When a military man takes over, it's very difficult to get rid of him. In spite of Menahem's appeasement of the Assyrians, they invaded Israel again and in the course of four campaigns (738, 734, 733, and 732) not only took a number of key cities but also captured much territory from Hamath and Naphtali in the north to Gilead and Galilee. The Assyrians also took Philistia as far south as Gaza, and even captured Damascus in Syria. Many Jews and Philistines were deported to Assyria. Pekah was slain by Hoshea, son of Elah, who was pro-Assyrian in his political views. We will hear more about Hoshea in 2 Kings 17. He reigned for nine years and was probably deported to Assyria where he died (17:1; 18:10-11).[10]

Jotham, a virtuous king (2 Kings 15:32-38; 2 Chron. 27)

Jotham, son of Uzziah, began to reign was he was twenty-five years old and ruled for sixteen years (27:1). He was coregent with his father after Uzziah was smitten with leprosy for invading the temple precincts. Jotham would be considered a good king, although his son Ahaz was a bad king. In fact, from Jotham, the eleventh king of Judah, to Zedekiah, the twentieth and last king of Judah, only Jotham, Hezekiah, and Josiah could be called good kings. That's three kings out of ten. The Lord kept David's lamp burning in Jerusalem all those years, but there came a time when He had to bring in the nation of Babylon and punish His people for their sins.

Like his father Uzziah, Jotham was both a builder and a warrior. He repaired the walls of Jerusalem and the Upper Gate of the temple. He also built cities in the Judean mountains and fortresses and towers in the wooded areas. His army confronted the armies of Israel and Syria, and he won a great victory over the Ammonites and put them under a very heavy annual tribute—nearly four tons of silver and 62,000 bushels each of wheat and barley (27:5). "So Jotham became mighty, because he prepared his ways before the Lord his God" (27:6, NKJV). We wonder how much more good he would have accomplished had he lived longer.

In Hebrew history we frequently find a godly father begetting an ungodly son and an ungodly father raising a godly son. Good king Jehoshaphat begat bad king Jehoram, but godly King Joash gave the nation a godly son (Amaziah), grandson (Uzziah), and great-grandson (Jotham). However, Jotham's son Ahaz was not a good king or a godly man, yet he begat good King Hezekiah, who in turn was the father of Manasseh, perhaps the most wicked king of the lot—and he had a reign of fifty-five years! Ezekiel the Prophet in Babylon dealt with this interesting phenomenon in chapter 18 of his prophecy.

God is sovereign in His gifts to individuals and nations. The Lord was longsuffering toward His people during those difficult and evil days, and He was faithful to keep His promises to David. But time was running out. After Ahaz died, only Hezekiah and Josiah would honor the Word of God and seek to obey His will. Yet, in spite of the sins and failings of the people, the Lord maintained a godly remnant in the nation, and from that godly remnant the Messiah would eventually be born.

"Known to God from eternity are all His works" (Acts 15:18, NKJV).

NINE

2 KINGS 16–17
[2 CHRONICLES 28]

A Tale of Two Kingdoms

An English proverb says, "Consider well who you are, where you came from, what you do and where you are going." The first two considerations were easily answered in both Israel and Judah, for both nations would have said, "We are God's chosen people, descendants of our father Abraham." As for the third question, both kings would have had to admit, "We do what our wicked predecessors did." King Ahaz of Judah didn't follow the godly example of his ancestor David, and Hoshea, king of Israel, imitated the wicked kings that ruled before him. They were free to make these decisions, *but they were not free to change the consequences of their decisions*, which brings us to the fourth question, "Where are you going?" For both rulers, God's answer was clear: "You and your people are plunging rapidly toward judgment and ruin." Solomon's words were about to be proved in both kingdoms: "Righteousness exalts a nation, but sin is a reproach to any people" (Prov. 14:34, NKJV).

Judah, a compromising nation (2 Kings 16:1-20; 2 Chron. 28:1-27)
Ahaz was the son of Jotham, a good king, and the father of Hezekiah, a very good king, but he himself was not a godly man

or even a good man. Instead of discovering and doing the will of God, Ahaz imitated the wicked kings of Israel and even the pagan practices of Assyria.[1] He even adopted the horrible worship practices of the pagan and sacrificed his son (2 Chron. 28:3 says "children," plural) to a pagan god, Baal or Molech, a practice that was clearly prohibited in the Law of Moses (Lev. 18:21; Deut. 18:10). Each Jewish son was to be redeemed by a sacrifice and therefore belonged to the Lord (Ex. 13; Num. 18:14-16). How could a son who belonged to God be sacrificed to an idol? But Ahaz was a compromiser both in his religious practices and his political leadership.

Political compromise (vv. 5-9; 2 Chron. 28:5-21). Pekah, the king of Israel, and Rezin, king of Syria, wanted Ahaz to join with them in opposing Assyria, but Ahaz refused because he was pro-Assyrian. In fact, he trusted Assyria instead of trusting the Lord. In retaliation, Syria and Israel planned to remove Ahaz from the throne and put their own puppet king in his place, but the Lord protected David's throne, even though Ahaz didn't deserve it. (For the complete story, read Isa. 7–9.)

According to 2 Chronicles 28:5-8, it was the Lord who brought these two kings against Judah, to punish Ahaz for his sins. Pehak and Rezin did a great deal of damage to Judah but they weren't able to take Jerusalem. One of the sons of Ahaz was killed, along with two key officers of state. The invading armies killed thousands of soldiers and took thousands of prisoners of war to Samaria. It looked like Israel was going to swallow up Judah!

The Lord raised up a prophet in Israel[2] who warned the Samaritan army that by taking these people of Judah as prisoners, Israel was breaking God's law and inviting God's judgment. After all, the people of Judah and the people of Samaria were part of one family, the family of Abraham. The Prophet Obed (not the same man as in 15:8) pointed out three sins the army of Israel committed. First, they were in a rage against the people of Judah and captured and killed them indiscriminately. Second, they planned to make slaves out of their own brothers and sisters, and this was contrary to God's law (Lev. 25:39ff). In doing these things, they showed no fear of the Lord and therefore were asking for Him to judge them (2 Chron. 28:9-11). Yes, God was angry with Judah (28:9, 25), but there was danger He would become angry at Israel for they way they treated Judah (28:11-13). After Obed's message, some of the leaders in Israel stood and affirmed what he had said and urged the army not to sin against the Lord and their brothers and sisters.

A remarkable thing happened: the people accepted God's message, repented, and changed their treatment of the prisoners. The Israelites not only fed and clothed them, and gave special help to the injured and feeble, but the soldiers even returned the loot they had taken from Judah. This was an instance of being "good Samaritans" on a national level (Luke 10:25-37), and it reminds us of Elisha's kindness to the Syrian soldiers who came to capture him (2 Kings 6:15-23). When the prisoners (with the spoils of battle) arrived back in Judah, they were living witnesses of the grace and goodness of the Lord, but there's no record that Ahaz led the nation in a great praise service.

This remarkable event carried another message to Judah: the time would come when the Babylonians would invade the land and take thousands of captives away to Babylon. This experience with the kingdom of Israel was somewhat of a "dress rehearsal" for the people of Judah, but Babylon wouldn't treat them as the Israelites did. Most of the Jewish captives would die in Babylon, and after seventy years, only a feeble remnant would return to rebuild the temple and try to establish the nation again.

Does the Lord still chasten nations today as He did in ancient days? The Jewish people, of course, belonged to a covenant nation, even though it was now divided into two kingdoms; and they were responsible to obey the covenant of the Lord. But what about the Gentile nations that have no covenant relationship with God? The Prophet Amos makes it clear that God knows the sins of the Gentile nations and holds them accountable (Amos 1-2). God never gave His law to the Gentiles (Ps. 147:19-20), but the demands of that law are written in the hearts of all people (Rom. 2:12-16), so the disobedient Gentiles are guilty before the Lord. As you read the Old Testament, you find God judging Sodom and Gomorrah (Gen. 18–19), Egypt (Ex. 1–14), the Gentile nations in and around Canaan (Num. 31–32; Joshua 1–12), and even Babylon (Jer. 50–51). However, because the Jews knew the true and living God and had the witness of His law, they were even more accountable. How tragic that apostate Israel and not enlightened Judah showed concern about obeying the message of God. Judah had the temple, the law, and the priesthood, but they didn't have the Lord. "Blessed is the nation whose God is the Lord" (Ps. 33:12).

Religious compromise (16:10-18; 2 Chron. 28:22-25). Not only did Israel and Syria attack Judah but God also brought the Edomites and the Philistines against Jerusalem. Ahaz sent word to the king of Assyria to come and help him. His message was that of a flattering flunky, what we today would call a "bootlicker." He called himself Tiglath-pileser's "servant" and "son," a strange posture for a descendant of David to take before a pagan ruler. To encourage the Assyrian king even more, Ahaz took wealth from the temple, the palace, and the princes and sent him a gift. Actually, Ahaz made Judah a vassal nation under the control and protection of Assyria. Ahaz had no living faith in the Lord and put his trust in the army of Assyria instead, and this cost him dearly. Indeed, Assyria did defeat Syria, but then Tiglath-pileser summoned his "son" and "servant" to Damascus to give an account of himself and to receive orders. Gone were the days when the kings of Judah and their armies were feared by the nations!

King Uzziah had tried to meddle with the ministry in the temple and the Lord gave him leprosy, but Urijah the high priest did anything the king commanded, even if it meant disobeying the Law of Moses. We aren't sure whether copying the pagan altar was wholly the idea of Ahaz or whether the king of Assyria commanded it. Perhaps Tiglath-pileser wanted this altar in the Jewish temple to remind the king and people of Judah that they were now under the authority of Assyria. Ahaz was not devoted to the faithful worship of Jehovah, so it's likely that this altar was copied simply to satisfy his pride. He would have a royal altar like the one in Damascus! Consequently, the God-designed altar of the Lord was shoved to one side.

All of this is a picture of what often happens in Christian ministries today: somebody sees something out in the world that would "fit" into the Lord's work, and the church starts to imitate the world. Moses was commanded to make the tabernacle according to what God showed him on the mount (Ex. 25:40; 26:30; Heb. 8:5), and likewise the temple was constructed according to the plans God gave to David (1 Chron. 28:11, 12, 19). The Jews didn't appoint a building committee and vote on the design. But today, the church is becoming so like the world that it's getting difficult to tell them apart. A. W. Tozer wrote,

> Aside from a few of the grosser sins, the sins of the unregenerated world are now approved by a shocking number of professedly "born-again" Christians, and copied eagerly. Young Christians take as their models the rankest kind of worldlings and try to be as much like them as possible. Religious leaders have adopted the techniques of the advertisers: boasting, baiting, and shameless exaggeration are now carried on as a normal procedure in church work. The moral climate is not that of the New Testament but that of Hollywood and Broadway.[3]

Ahaz thought that the Lord would be pleased with sacrifices offered on this magnificent new altar, but he was wrong. The Lord doesn't want sacrifice; He wants obedience (1 Sam. 15:22-23); and Ahaz worshiped the gods of the heathen nations (2 Chron. 28:23). No fire from heaven ignited the sacrifices placed on that pagan altar (Lev. 9:24), because the Lord had rejected it. The religious novelties in churches today may excite and entertain the people, but they don't edify the church or exalt the Lord. The sanctuary becomes a theater, worship becomes entertainment, ministry becomes performance, and a congregation becomes an audience. The measure of all this is not the glory of God but the applause of the people.

But replacing God's altar with a pagan altar was just the beginning. King Ahaz also "remodeled" the laver and the ten movable stands that held the ten basins for preparing sacrifices (1 Chron. 28:17; 1 Kings 7:23-40). Apparently he needed the precious metal for his own purposes, so he took it from the Lord. But to please the king of Assyria, Ahaz had to remove his own royal entryway to the temple as well as the royal canopy (or dais for his throne) that he had placed in the temple. Tihglath-pileser was now in charge, not King Ahaz,

However, the king could never have made all these changes without the cooperation of Urijah, the high priest (16:10, 11, 15, 16). When King Uzziah tried to rebel against the Word of the Lord and enter the temple, the high priest Azariah with eighty other priests successfully withstood him (2 Chron. 26:16ff); but Urijah and his priests compromised, disobeyed the Law of Moses and gave in to their king. Once compromise begins, it continues to grow; and all that it takes for evil to triumph is for weak people like Urijah to let leaders have their way. Ahaz not only replaced the altar and removed metal from the furnishings, but he finally took all the vessels for himself, closed the doors of the temple, and set up altars in the streets of Jerusalem (2 Chron. 28:24-25). "Do you not know that a little leaven leavens the whole lump of dough?" (1 Cor. 5:6, NASB; see Gal. 5:9). Once we allow worldliness to get into the church fellowship, it will quietly grow, pollute the fellowship and eventually take over. It was not until the reign of his son Hezekiah that the temple Ahaz defiled was reopened and sanctified for ministry (2 Chron. 29:1-29).

When Ahaz died, he was buried in Jerusalem but not in the royal tombs (16:19-20; 28:26-27). In this, he joined Jehoram (2 Chron. 21:20), Joash (24:25), and Uzziah (26:23), and Manasseh would join them (33:20). The unbelief and unfaithfulness of Ahaz did great damage to the kingdom of Judah, some of which his son Hezekiah would be able to repair.

Israel, a captive nation (2 Kings 17:1-41; 18:9-12)

Hoshea was the last ruler of the northern kingdom of Israel, for in his day (722 B.C.), the Assyrians invaded the land, deported many of the citizens, and repopulated Israel with Gentile peoples from lands Assyria had conquered. The kingdom of Israel became Samaria, named after the capital city, and it was a nation whose citizens were not pure Jews but a commingling of many ethnic strains.

God had given His people so many blessings, and now those blessings would fall into the hands of Assyria and Babylon. The Jews had a living Lord, but they replaced Him with dead idols. Their wealthy land was confiscated by enemy nations, the people were taken captive, and eventually Jerusalem and the temple were destroyed (586 B.C.). God in His mercy preserved a faithful remnant so a light would remain shining and He could fulfill the promises He had made to His people.

Israel lost their leader (17:1-5). Hoshea had assassinated Pekah and seized the throne of Israel (15:29-31). Tiglath-pileser had died and Shalmaneser V was now king of Assyria, and Hoshea gave homage to him and brought him tribute. However, Hoshea secretly made a treaty with Egypt to enlist them to fight for Israel and help them break the Assyrian yoke.[4] Ever since Abraham fled to Egypt to escape a famine and only got himself and his wife into trouble (Gen. 12:10ff), various Jewish leaders have vainly looked to Egypt for help. (See Gen. 26:2; Num. 14:1-4; Deut. 17:16; Isa. 30:1-2; 31:1.) So it is with believers today who turn to the world for help instead of waiting on the Lord and trusting Him. When Shalmaneser discovered the plot, he took Hoshea prisoner and left the throne of Israel empty.[5]

In 725, Shalmaneser began to besiege Samaria, but then he died (or was killed) and his leading general, Sargon II, took over. The siege lasted three years, and in 722, the city capitulated. Assyria had already taken the tribes east of the Jordan (1 Chron. 5:24-26), so now they possessed everything but Judah, and that would fall to Babylon.

Israel lost their land (v. 6; 18:9-12). As we have seen, Assyria's policy was to relocate conquered peoples and replace them with prisoners from other nations.[6] It was clearly stated in God's covenant with His people that their disobedience would bring defeat in war (Deut. 28:25, 49-50, 52), oppression and slavery (Deut. 28:29, 33, 48, 68) and captivity (Deut. 28:36, 43, 63-68); and all of this happened to both Israel and Judah. The land belonged to the Lord (Lev. 25:2, 23, 38) and the people were His "tenants." Not only was the land His, but so were the people (Lev. 25:55). They would possess the land and enjoy its blessings as long as they kept the terms of the covenant, but repeated disobedience would bring discipline *within* the land and ultimately discipline *outside* the land. That's exactly what happened. Because of the people's sins during the period of the judges, seven different nations invaded the land, took the crops, and enslaved the people right in their own land. After the division of the nation, Israel was taken captive by Assyria and Judah by Babylon. God kept the terms of His covenant.

Israel disobeyed their law (vv. 7-17). These verses read like a legal court case against northern kingdom of Israel. The law was a gift from God, an agreement that guaranteed His provision and protection if the people did His will. But they forgot how God had delivered them from Egypt and set them free. They ignored the Law of Moses that commanded them not to worship false gods but to destroy the heathen idols, temples, and shrines (Deut. 7, 13). Israel began with secret worship of idols (v. 9), but this eventually became public, and Jehovah was acknowledged as one god among many. The Lord sent prophets who admonished and warned the people, but the people paid little attention.

As their ancestors had done so many times, the Jewish people stiffened their necks and hardened their hearts and refused to obey the Lord (Deut. 9:6, 13; 10:12-22; Neh. 9:16, 17, 29; Ps. 106). Since we become like the god we worship (Ps. 115:8), the people became "vanity" (emptiness, nothingness) because they worshiped vain idols (v. 15). In fact, they turned to idols and made a golden calf while Moses was communing with God on

Mount Sinai (Ex. 32). After the division of the kingdom, King Jeroboam made *two* golden calves for the people to worship (1 Kings 12:25ff). As is often the case, it is the children who suffer for the sins of the parents, for the Jewish fathers began to offer their sons and daughters on the fiery altars of the heathen gods. *Israel angered their Lord (vv. 18-33)*. The anger of the Lord is His holy wrath; it must not be compared to a child's temper tantrum. The Lord was longsuffering toward His people and made ample provision to bring them back to Himself, but they refused. God's wrath is anger motivated by love, which is anguish. It's the anguish of a father who wants the best for his children, but they prefer to go their own way. These verses inform us that the division of the kingdom into Judah and Israel was an act of God as He sought to protect David's dynasty from the idolatry in Israel. However, King Jereboam's false, manmade religion infected Judah, and it was only by the grace of God that a faithful remnant remained.

The phrase "to fear the Lord" means "to worship the Lord according to the Law of Moses" (vv. 25, 28, 32, 34). The mixture of religions among the various peoples resulted in what we today would call "pluralism." At first, the Jews didn't worship God at all, and He disciplined them for their unfaithfulness (v. 25). The Jewish people worshiped Jehovah *plus the gods of the other nations*. God will not share worship with false gods, so it's no wonder He became angry. All the people in the land should have repented, turned from their false gods, and turned to the Lord; but instead, the Lord's people accepted the false gods of other nations.

The king of Assyria believed that each god was associated with the land from which the people came, and therefore the new residents didn't know how to worship the Lord of Israel. They could never learn from the Israelites left behind because they had been worshiping the golden calves since the days of King Jeroboam. The king of Assyria ordered one of the Jewish priests to be sent to Israel to teach the people how to worship "the god of the land." But this priest went to Bethel, the site of one of the shrines dedicated to the golden calf! How much he knew about the true

Jewish faith and what he taught aren't revealed to us, but the situation doesn't appear to be encouraging.

Many people today would applaud this "world congress of religions," but the Lord abhors it. In a democracy, we learn to accept pluralism, but this doesn't mean we approve of it or believe that all religions are equal. In the United States, all religions are equal before the law and may be freely practiced, but Christians still believe that "there is no other name under heaven given among men by which we must be saved (Acts 4:12, NKJV). Jesus rejected the Samaritan religion because "salvation is of the Jews" (John 4:19-24). The Jewish people who were left in the land appointed their own priests and ignored the standards established by God through Moses (v. 32). The people set up their own religious ceremonies and integrated with this new system some of the beliefs of their new neighbors. There was something for everybody, and it didn't matter what you believed or how you worshiped, just as long as you were religious (vv. 29-33). Does this sound familiar?

Israel did not learn her lesson (vv. 34-41). It's often been said that the one thing we learn from history is that we don't learn from history. In spite of the way the Lord had warned them and chastened them, the people continued to worship the Lord along with the other gods, and they did it their own way. They ignored their history as the people of God delivered from Egyptian bondage. They forgot God's laws and covenants, especially God's commandments concerning idolatry (Ex. 20:1-6). Like many professed Christians today, the people of Israel worshiped the Lord where and how they pleased, but they also paid respect to the false gods of the other nations.

What finally happened to these ten disobedient tribes? We hear about "the ten lost tribes of Israel," but the Bible never uses that phrase. Many people in the ten tribes assimilated with the peoples brought into the land by the Assyrians, and this produced the Samaritan people. But there's no evidence in Scripture that the ten tribes of Israel are "lost." Long before the Assyrians captured the Northern Kingdom, dedicated people from the ten tribes moved to Judah and remained faithful to the Lord (1 Kings

12:16-20; 2 Chron. 11:5-16; 19:4-10). Godly King Hezekiah invited true believers to come to Judah and worship God according to the Scriptures, and many of them came (2 Chron. 30:1-14, 25-27). Josiah's reforms had a tremendous effect on the Jewish people (2 Chron. 34:1-7, 33; 35:17-19). Though Jesus spoke about "the lost sheep of the house of Israel" (Matt. 10:5-6), the New Testament knows nothing about any "lost tribes of Israel." (See Matt. 4:12-16 and Luke 2:36-38.) Paul spoke about "our twelve tribes" (Acts 26:7) and James wrote his epistle "to the twelve tribes scattered abroad" (James 1:1). If we take Revelation 7:1-8 literally, then in the last days the Lord will find people from the tribes of Israel.

The main message from this tragic chapter is that false worship leads to corrupt practices, and corrupt practices result in divine condemnation and judgment. Disobedient and compromising leaders—both kings and priests—failed to teach the people the Word of God, and as each new generation came along, the nation drifted further from the Lord. There came a day when God's anger was displayed against His people, and that was the end of the political entity known as Israel, the Northern Kingdom.

TEN

The Making of a King—Part I

The name Hezekiah means "the Lord strengthens," and during his reign of twenty-nine years (715–687), King Hezekiah needed God's strength to accomplish all that he did. Like Asa (1 Kings 15:11), Jehoshaphat (22:43), and Josiah (2 Kings 22:2), his model was King David, which means that, while Hezekiah wasn't perfect, he did seek to obey the Lord and please Him. He was one of the few kings who actually removed the high places and put an end to idol worship in the hills. He restored temple worship and encouraged the people from both Judah and Israel to come to the temple in Jerusalem and worship the Lord. The Lord had commanded that there be one central place of worship, and that was at Jerusalem (Deut. 12).

The sequence of events in Hezekiah's life as recorded in Scripture is not strictly chronological. Most students agree that the events recorded in Isaiah 38 and 39—his illness and his welcome of the Babylonian ambassadors—actually antedated the Assyrian invasion (Isa. 36–37). We will take this approach as we study Hezekiah's life and ministry and seek to integrate the material in Kings, Chronicles, and Isaiah.

Hezekiah the reformer (2 Kings 18:4; 2 Chron. 29:3–31:21)
It's interesting that 2 Kings has but one verse describing Hezekiah's reforms (18:4), while 2 Chronicles devotes three chapters to this important part of his life. However, 2 Kings mentions how King Hezekiah destroyed the bronze serpent made by Moses (Num. 21:5-9), but this isn't mentioned in Chronicles. The serpent was a religious relic that had reached the status of an idol. "Nehushstan" probably means "a piece of bronze, a brass thing." How easy it is for human nature to want to honor religious relics that have no power! Hezekiah was a man of faith who trusted the living God and followed His law, and he didn't want the people worshiping a dead, useless image.

He cleansed the temple (29:3-19). Hezekiah didn't waste any time getting Judah back to the worship of the true and living God. His father Ahaz had defiled the temple and finally closed the doors and stopped the Levitical ministry (28:24). Hezekiah commanded the priests to sanctify themselves so they would be able to cleanse the temple and restore the worship that the Lord had commanded through Moses. The abandoning of the temple worship by the people of the Northern Kingdom had led to their captivity, and the defiling and neglecting of the temple by Ahaz had brought discipline to Judah, including invasions by Syria, Edom, and Philistia. The temple worship was at the heart of the Jewish nation, and if that was wrong, everything else would be wrong.

But Hezekiah wasn't interested in a mere housecleaning project, because he had it in his heart not only to rededicate the temple and the people but also to enter into a covenant with the Lord (v. 10). Fourteen leaders are named in verses 12-14, men who set the example and led the way for a new beginning for temple ministry. If the spiritual leaders aren't right with God, how can He bless His people? All three Levitical families were represented—Mahath and Joel from the Kohathites, Kish and Azariah from Marari, and Joah and Eden from the Gershonites (see Num. 3–4). The clan of Elizaphan belonged to the Kohathites (Num. 3:30) and had achieved an honorable reputation because of their faithful service. They were represented by Shimri and Juel. The other men listed were among the temple singers related to Asaph (from Gershon), Heman (from Kohath) or Jeduthun (from Merari), well-known musicians, singers, and worship leaders. King Hezekiah knew that there had to be music and praise or the temple worship would displease the Lord. These leaders and their helpers sanctified themselves before the Lord so that He could use them to sanctify His temple.

On the first day of the first month, they began to cleanse the temple, beginning in the Holy of Holies and the Holy Place. They carried out the accumulated trash and remnants of idolatrous worship, took it down to the Kidron Valley, and burned it. After sanctifying the building they cleansed the porch. This included removing the pagan altar that Ahaz had built, and placing the Lord's altar where it belonged (2 Kings 16:10ff). The Levites also cleansed the vessels and instruments used in the temple services and put them in their proper places. It took sixteen days to complete the work, which meant they missed Passover, which was on the fourteenth day of the first month. However, Hezekiah held a great Passover during the second month (ch. 30).

If we are to have revival in the Lord's work, we must begin with cleansing. Over the years, individuals and churches can gradually accumulate a great deal of "religious rubbish" while ignoring the essentials of spiritual worship. It's not by doing some unique new thing that we experience new blessing from the Lord, but by returning to the "old things" and doing them well. If we confess our sins (2 Chron. 7:14), light the lamps, burn the incense (a picture of prayer, Ps. 141:1-2), and offer ourselves as living sacrifices (v. 7; Rom. 12:1-2), the Lord will see and hear and will send His blessing.

He consecrated the temple (vv. 20-36). The king and the rulers of the city met together at the temple and offered sacrifices to the Lord. They brought sacrifices for the kingdom (Judah and Israel), the temple, and the kingdom of Judah in particular. The sin offerings were offered to atone for the sins of the people, and the

BE DISTINCT

priests included both Israel and Judah (v. 24—"all Israel"). The burnt offerings symbolized total dedication to the Lord. As the sacrifices were being offering to the Lord, the musicians and singers offered their praise to the Lord, following David's instructions, using David's songs, and playing David's instruments (vv. 25-27, 30; 1 Chron. 23:5-6).

But this wasn't a dedication service planned only for the king and his leaders, for the people in the congregation sanctified themselves and brought their offerings as well (vv. 28-36). They brought a large number of sacrifices, including three thousand sheep, which were probably given as fellowship offerings. Part of the fellowship offering was kept by the worshiper and eaten with his family as a fellowship meal. Hezekiah was following the example of Solomon when he dedicated the temple more than two hundred years before (1 Kings 8:62ff). It was a time of great rejoicing for the king and his people. Keep in mind that many devout people from the apostate northern kingdom of Israel (now Samaria) had fled to Judah so they could worship the Lord according to the Law of Moses, so this dedication service involved all the tribes.

He celebrated Passover (30:1-27). Three times each year, the Jewish men were required to go to Jerusalem to celebrate the feasts of Passover, Pentecost, and Tabernacles (Ex. 23:14-17; 34:22-24). To the Christian believer today, Passover speaks of the death of Christ, the Lamb of God who died for us (1 Cor. 5:7; John 1:29). On Pentecost, the Holy Spirit came upon the early church (Acts 2); and Tabernacles speaks of the future kingdom when Jesus shall reign and we shall reign with Him (Zech. 14). Passover commemorated the release of the Jewish people from Egyptian bondage, so it was a national celebration. For this reason, Hezekiah invited Jews from both Judah and Israel (Samaria) to come to Jerusalem for the feast. The Law of Moses made provision for celebrating the Passover in the second month (Num. 9:6-13), and Hezekiah took advantage of this provision. Neither the temple nor the priests and Levites had been ready the first month (vv. 1-3).

The emphasis in the invitation was on "all Israel" (vv. 5-6) and not just the people of Judah. Since the days of Solomon, there had not been a Passover involving the entire nation, and Hezekiah wanted to unite the people spiritually even though they were divided politically. The Northern Kingdom (Samaria) was under the rule of Assyria and the Jewish remnant living there worshiped the gods of the Gentile nations. They needed to return to the God of Abraham, Isaac, and Jacob (v. 6). The Jewish people had a common ancestry and a common worship, and it was time to put the Lord first, forget past differences and celebrate. The repeated words "turn again" and "return" reveal the desire of Hezekiah's heart (vv. 6, 9). If the people all turned in repentance to God, God would return to bless His people. Hezekiah built his appeal around the words of Solomon in 2 Chronicles 7:14.

Alas, the remnant in bondage to Assyria was just as stiff-necked as their ancestors were when God dealt with them in the wilderness. Here was an opportunity to make a new beginning and glorify the Lord by seeking His compassion, grace and mercy (v. 9), but most of the people outside Judah rejected the invitation. They mocked Hezekiah's words and laughed at his messengers, but so doing, they rejected the blessing the Lord had for them. However, there were some people who had the courage to disagree with their families and friends and go to Jerusalem for the feast, among them men from the northern tribes of Asher, Manasseh, and Zebulun. They came a long distance with humble hearts, seeking the blessing of the Lord. God gave the worshipers who gathered oneness of mind and heart so that it was the Lord who was the center of the event and not some political agenda.

The celebration is described in 30:13-27. The people removed the altars that King Ahaz had put up in Jerusalem (v. 14), for there could be no united worship unless they met at the one appointed altar in the temple court. What a paradox that the people were eager to worship the Lord, but the priests and Levites were ceremonially unclean and therefore unable to minister at the altar! But they remedied the situation and brought the burnt offerings that were to be offered daily (Ex. 29:38-43; Num. 28:1-8). During the reign of King Ahaz, the appointed temple services had been stopped, and the priests allowed themselves to become disqualified to serve at the altar; but between Hezekiah's accession to the throne and the celebration of the Passover, there had been time for them to prepare themselves.

But many common people in the large congregation were also unclean (Ex. 12:14-16; 13:6-10), perhaps because they had left their homes quickly or because they had been defiled during the journey to Jerusalem (Num. 9:9-10). But Hezekiah knew that God was concerned about the hearts of the worshipers and not the details of meeting ceremonial requirements, and he prayed that God would cleanse and accept them (1 Sam. 15:22-23; Isa. 1:10-17; Hoses 6:6; Micah 6:6-8; Mark 12:32-33). God answered his prayer, because it's the heart that God wants and not mere religious ritual. If there were any legalists in the congregation, they must have been very upset, but their attitude would only rob them of God's blessing. (See Luke 18:9-14 and Ps. 51:10-11 and 15-16.) If God's people today would prepare their hearts for worship with as much care as they prepare their "Sunday best," the Lord would send His blessings on His church.

There was so much joy and blessings that Hezekiah and the people decided to continue the celebration for another week, and the king generously provided the sacrifices needed for the offerings, and this provided food for the people. The king's example motivated the leaders of Judah to bring extra sacrifices as well, so there was plenty of food for everybody. Spontaneous giving comes from spontaneous worship of the Lord and heartfelt gratitude to Him. When Solomon dedicated the temple, he also kept the people there another week (7:8-9).

He commenced and organized the temple ministry (31:1-21). When the second week of the feast ended, before the people left for home, the priests pronounced the benediction God commanded them to give in Numbers 6:22-27, and the worshipers left Jerusalem with the blessing of the Lord upon them. But as they carried the blessing home, they also obeyed the Lord and destroyed the idols in Judah, Benjamin, Ephraim, and Manasseh. It's one thing to have an exciting time praising God in a two-week special meeting, but it's quite something else to return home afterward and live like people who have met the Lord. King Hezekiah knew that the blessings of the Passover feast wouldn't continue unless the people could participate in the regular ministry at the temple. It's wonderful to have a great feast at Christmas or on some special anniversary, but you can't live all year on one or two special meals. For that reason, Hezekiah followed David's instructions (1 Chron. 23–26) and organized the priests and Levites for ministry at the temple. He set a good example by providing from his own flocks and herds the sacrifices needed day by day and month by month. King Hezekiah sought the Lord and did everything for Him from his heart (v. 21).

After staffing and organizing the temple ministry, Hezekiah also admonished the people to bring their tithes and offerings to the temple for the support of the priests and Levites (v. 4; Num. 18:8-32; Deut. 12:1-19; 14:22-29). He allocated special chambers in the temple for storing the gifts and he appointed faithful men to oversee the distribution of the food. The priests and Levites depended on these gifts for their own support and that of their families (see Neh. 13:1-14). The king seemed especially concerned about the little children who had been weaned (vv. 16, 18). He wanted none of God's servants or their families to go hungry.

In the third month (May/June), the time of grain harvest, the people brought the grain and the priests and Levites heaped it up. During the seventh month (Sept./Oct.), when the orchard and vineyard harvests came in, these gifts of fruits and wine were added to the store. Like the gifts brought for the building of the tabernacle (Ex. 36:5-7) and the construction of the temple (1 Chron. 29:1-20), the tithes and offerings brought to the newly consecrated temple were far more than the king expected. A worshiping people will always be a generous people, especially when their leaders set the example, and Judah was no exception.

Hezekiah the negotiator (2 Kings 18:7-16)
Judah had been a vassal state under Assyria since the reign of
King Ahaz, Hezekiah's father (16:7-18). When Sargon, ruler of
Assyria, died in battle, and Sennacherib took the throne, it
seemed to Hezekiah an opportune time to break that yoke.
Sennacherib was involved in other empire concerns, so Hezekiah
didn't send him the annual tribute. Judah had been victorious
over the Philistines, so the kingdom was feeling strong. In 722
B.C., Assyria attacked Israel and captured the city of Samaria, and
this meant that the Assyrian army was now right next door to
Judah.
   In 715 B.C., Sennacherib invaded Judah and headed toward
Jerusalem.[1] Hezekiah's faith was very weak, so he humbled himself before the king and paid the tribute money that he owed—
eleven tons of silver and one ton of gold. Some of the wealth
came from the king's own treasure, but it's disappointing to see
that Hezekiah took the rest of it from the temple of the Lord. He
followed the bad example of his father (16:8). King David didn't
negotiate with his enemies or try to buy them off; he attacked
and defeated them. Of course, Sennacherib withdrew from
Judah, but he had every intention of returning.

**Hezekiah the sufferer (2 Kings 20:1-11; 2 Chron. 32:24-26; Isa.
38:1-8)**
According to the chronologers, this is the next important event
in the life of Hezekiah. It took place fifteen years before his death
in 687, so his sickness and healing, as well as the visit of the
Babylonian ambassadors, occurred in the year 702 B.C.. The next
year, the Assyrians returned and attacked Jerusalem.
   Did the Lord send this sickness to discipline Hezekiah because
he compromised with the Assyrians? The record in 2 Chronicles
32:24 tells us that the king had become proud and this was one
way that the Lord humbled him. The fact that the Prophet Isaiah
visited him with such a solemn message indicates how serious
this experience really was, for the king was going to die. "Set your

house in order" involved most of all appointing an heir to the throne. Hezekiah had become king at the age of twenty-five (2 Kings 18:1) and died in 687. His son Manasseh became king in 687 at the age of twenty-two, which means he was born in 709, so he would have been seven years old when Isaiah told his father he was going to die. Joash had ascended the throne at the age of seven (11:4ff), but he had Jehoiada the godly priest to advise him. Obviously, the throne of David was in jeopardy.

Hezekiah's response was to turn away from all around him and pray to the Lord.[2] If his statement in 20:3 and Isaiah 38:2 sounds like boasting, keep in mind that Hezekiah was only claiming the promise of 2 Chronicles 6:16-17. This promise was part of the Lord's gracious covenant with David and his descendants (2 Sam. 7:1-17), and Hezekiah was simply reminding the Lord that he had been faithful to obey His law. In other words, as a faithful son of David, he was "qualified" to live. God's message to the king through Isaiah emphasized the importance of King David and the continuation of his descendants on the throne in Jerusalem.

God answered Hezekiah's prayer by telling Isaiah how to bring about healing and also by giving Isaiah two great promises to share with Hezekiah. First, the king would recover and worship at the temple within three days; and second, if the Assyrians returned, the Lord would defend and deliver the city of Jerusalem. Remember, Hezekiah's illness occurred *before* the second invasion of Sennacherib's army. To assure the king of the truth of these promises, God gave him a miraculous sign: the shadow on the steps of Ahaz (a large sundial) went backward ten degrees. As the sun went down, the shadow would naturally get longer, but suddenly, the shadow became shorter. Did God reverse the movement of planet earth or simply cause the shadow itself to go back on the steps? God doesn't explain His miracles and it's unwise for us to do it for Him.

God disciplines us because He loves us and wants to prevent us from disobeying Him and losing His blessing (Heb. 12:1-11). Chastening isn't the work of a stern judge as he punishes a criminal. It's the ministry of a loving father as he seeks to bring out the very best in his children, for the Father wants us to be "conformed to the image of His Son" (Rom. 8:29, NKJV)

Hezekiah the singer (Isa. 38:9-22)

The Prophet Isaiah recorded the psalm Hezekiah wrote after he had been healed and given fifteen more years of life (Isa. 38:9-20). It's likely that Hezekiah wrote other psalms as well (see v. 20, KJV and NASB) because we read about "the men of Hezekiah" in Proverbs 25:1. This title suggests that the king had a special "guild" of scholars who worked with the Scriptures and copied the manuscripts.[3] The psalm that Hezekiah wrote in commemoration of his sickness and deliverance certainly is filled with vivid imagery that teaches us a great deal about life and death. This is especially true in the NIV translation.

Hezekiah saw life as a journey that ended at the gates of death, or "Sheol," the Hebrew word for the realm of the dead (v. 10). He was in the prime of his life and yet was being robbed of the rest of his years. (He was probably thirty-seven or thirty-eight years old.) Perhaps he was thinking of Psalm 139:16 where David declares that God has written in His book the number of each person's days. Hezekiah lamented that he was leaving the land of the living and would see his friends no more.[4] Keep in mind that the full light had not yet been given concerning immortality, the intermediate world, and the Resurrection (2 Tim. 1:10).

But death is not only the end of a journey; it's also like taking down a tent (v. 12). Paul used the tent image in a similar way (2 Cor. 5:1-4) and so did Peter (2 Peter 1:13-14). But Hezekiah also pictures his impending death as a weaving being taken off the loom (v. 12). God "wove us" in our mother's womb (Ps. 139:13-16) before birth, and during our lives, He wanted to weave us into something beautiful and useful for His glory. Hezekiah was being cut off before the pattern was completed. Day and night, the king was in anxiety and suffering, like a helpless bird being attacked by a hungry lion (vv. 13-14). All he could do was mourn like a dove or cry out like a thrush or a swift.

In verse 15, the atmosphere changes and he gives thanks to God for His mercy in rescuing him from the pit (vv. 17-18). God not only saved his life, but He cleansed his record and put his sins behind His back (v. 17; see Isa. 43:25; Micah 7:19). The Lord had disciplined the king because of his pride (2 Chron. 32:24), but now the king promised to "walk humbly" for the rest of his life (v. 15). Hezekiah dedicated himself to praising the Lord and telling the next generation what the Lord had done for him. Perhaps that's when he organized "the men of Hezekiah" so that the biblical manuscripts would be carefully copied and protected.

However, Hezekiah's pride reared its ugly head again and the king once more had to be rebuked.

ELEVEN

2 KINGS 18:17–19:37; 20:12-21
[2 CHRONICLES 32:27-33; ISAIAH 36–37; 39]

The Making of a King—Part II

We have seen King Hezekiah as an effective reformer who cleansed and consecrated the temple and restored the priestly ministry. But Hezekiah the negotiator capitulated to Assyria and paid tribute in order to avoid war. Then God sent a severe illness to Hezekiah to humble him and he cried out to God for mercy. Following that victory, Hezekiah stumbled again by welcoming the Babylonian envoys and showing them what they had no right to see. This was not a praiseworthy hour in Hezekiah's life.

Hezekiah the boaster (2 Kings 20:12-19; 2 Chron. 32:27-31; Isa. 39)
Scripture pictures our adversary the Devil as a serpent and a lion (Gen. 3:1ff; 2 Cor. 11:1-4; 1 Peter 5:8-9). Satan usually comes first as a serpent to deceive us, but if that doesn't work, he returns as a lion to devour us. This was Hezekiah's experience. First the Babylonian ambassadors came to Jerusalem to learn how wealthy and strong Judah was, and then the Assyrian army came to ravage the land, capture Jerusalem, and deport the Jewish people to Assyria. The ambassadors deceived Hezekiah because he didn't seek God's wisdom from Isaiah the prophet, but the king did seek

the Lord when the Assyrians invaded the land, and the Lord gave him victory.

Hezekiah's pride (20:12-13; 32:27-30; 39:1-2). We have already learned that Hezekiah had a problem with pride (2 Chron. 32:25-26). His near-fatal sickness did humble him, but the visit of the Babylonian envoys made it clear that the old sin was still very much alive. The envoys came to Judah with two purposes in mind: (1) to find out how strong the kingdom was, and (2) to try to influence Hezekiah to unite with Babylon in opposing Assyria. Because he didn't fully grasp their true purpose, Hezekiah assumed that it was a great honor to be visited by officials from the king of Babylon. At that time in history, Assyria was the strongest empire and Babylon was an empire on the rise. Why should Hezekiah worry about Babylon? Because one day Assyria would move off the scene and Babylon would be the key nation in the Near East. From 606 to 586, Babylon would invade Judah, destroy Jerusalem and the temple, and take the nation into captivity. Babylon first came as the serpent, then she returned as the lion.

The envoys brought expensive gifts from the king of Babylon as well as personal letters expressing his pleasure that Hezekiah had recovered from his dangerous illness. Hezekiah should have realized that Merodach-Beladan had no personal interest in the health of the king of Judah but only wanted to obligate Hezekiah to become an ally of Babylon. It's likely that the envoys helped to inflate Hezekiah's ego by complimenting him on his military resources and personal wealth. (See 2 Chron. 32:27-30.) Foolishly, Hezekiah gave them the grand tour and showed them his treasures and weapons. It appears that Hezekiah was better at managing his scribes and writing his psalms than he was at overseeing the politics of the kingdom. All that Hezekiah possessed came from the hand of God and belonged to God, so why should Hezekiah boast about it? He may have made a good impression on the envoys but he grieved the Lord and endangered the kingdom and the city.

Pride is one of Satan's chief weapons in his battle against the Lord and His people. Satan himself committed the sin of pride when he rebelled against God and sought the worship and obedience that God alone deserves (Isa. 14:12-15). Pride makes us rob God of the glory that belongs to Him alone. Pride gives us a feeling of false security and this leads us into sin and defeat. Charles Spurgeon said to his London congregation, "Be not proud of race, face, place, or grace." Good advice! William Barclay wrote, "Pride is the ground in which all the other sins grow, and the parent from which all the other sins come."

Isaiah's prophecy (20:14-18; 29:3-8). Hezekiah should have conferred with Isaiah as soon as the diplomatic pouch arrived with news that the Babylonian envoys were coming to Jerusalem. When the prophet heard that a foreign entourage had come and gone, he went to the king and asked two important questions: "What did they say and where did they come from?" The king never did answer the first question, but he did admit that the men had come from Babylon. That envoys should come to Judah from "a far country" obviously pleased the king, and no doubt he was pleased to find an ally in the battle against Assyria.

As you read the Book of Isaiah, you soon discover that the prophet already knew something about the future of Babylon (see 13–14 and 20:1-10). At that time in history, most people would have pointed to Assyria as the threatening world power, for Babylon was just starting to get recognition on the world scene. Assyria had defeated the kingdom of Israel, but it would be Babylon that would conquer the kingdom of Judah, and Isaiah 39:5-7 is Isaiah's first clear prophecy of that event. A century after Hezekiah's death, Babylon would destroy Jerusalem and the temple, and some of Hezekiah's descendants would go into captivity and his wealth carried to Babylon.

The Lord's patience (20:19). Hezekiah's response wasn't a sigh of relief that his generation had escaped judgment, but rather was an expression of his acceptance of the will of God. Hezekiah's pride had been broken once again (2 Chron. 32:26), but for the sake of the nation and the throne of David, he was grateful there would be peace. The Lord had been longsuffering toward Hezekiah and the king didn't realize that another great trial was about to begin—Assyria's assault against Jerusalem. However, the king had learned some valuable lessons from his sickness and his mishandling of the affair of the Babylonian envoys. How gracious it is of the Lord to prepare us for what He has prepared for us!

Hezekiah the commander (18:17-37; 2 Chron. 32:1-19; Isa. 36)
"After these deeds of faithfulness, Sennacherib king of Assyria came and entered Judah" (2 Chron. 32:1, NKJV). The "deeds of faithfulness" were Hezekiah's labors to cleanse and consecrate the temple, the priests, and the Levites, and to restore true worship in Judah. One would think that God would reward his service by giving him peace, but instead, the Lord allowed the Assyrians to return to Judah and threaten Jerusalem. Hezekiah was faithful to the Lord, but it seems as though the Lord wasn't faithful to Hezekiah. After all, the king had done "that which was good and right and truth before the Lord his God" (2 Chron. 31:20) and had done it "with all his heart" (v. 21). Why, then, didn't the Lord protect Judah from another invasion?

"It is the standing puzzle of the Old Testament," said Alexander Maclaren, "how good men come to be troubled, and how bad men come to be prosperous."[1] We have little trouble understanding why the Assyrians destroyed the northern kingdom of Israel; after all, the nation was worshiping idols and rebelling against the law of God. But Judah had returned to the Lord under Hezekiah's leadership, and though the king had made some mistakes, his heart was sincere before God. But God had His divine purposes to fulfill in Hezekiah's life and in the life of the nation. It was an easy thing for God to send an angel to destroy 185,000 Assyrian soldiers, but it was much more difficult to work with King Hezekiah and transform him into a man of faith. When we allow God to have His way, the trials of life work *for* us and not *against* us, and they bring great glory to the Lord. The king needed to learn that he was second in command (see Josh. 5:13-15) and that the Lord alone was sovereign.

The preparation (2 Chron. 32:1-8). Hezekiah knew that the Assyrians were coming, so he met with his leaders and took steps to strengthen Jerusalem. By working with his leaders he united them in sympathy and strategy, an important factor for leadership in war. The Assyrian records state that their army took forty-six fortified cities in Judah before settling in Lachish and planning the siege of Jerusalem. By blocking up the water supply outside the city, Hezekiah prevented the invaders from having ample supplies of fresh water. Hezekiah had already dug the tunnel between the Gihon spring and the city of Jerusalem (2 Kings 20:20) so that the people in the city would not die of thirst. Even today, this tunnel is a popular place for visitors to the Holy Land. Hezekiah also had the wall of Jerusalem repaired and strengthened, and he put extra towers on it. He even constructed a second outside wall and then strengthened the "Millo," the terraces that butted up against the walls (see 11:8; 1 Kings 11:27). He organized the army, appointed officers, gave them weapons, and then encouraged them by making a speech. His address reflected the words of Moses to Israel and to Joshua (Deut. 31:1-8) and God's words to Joshua (Josh. 1:1-9; see also 2 Kings 6:16). Hezekiah was wise to use God's Word to encourage his soldiers and remind them of the past victories of God's people because they had trusted the Lord.

The confrontation (18:17-18; 36:1-3). Hezekiah's near-fatal illness occurred in 702 B.C. and so did the visit of the Babylonian envoys. This means that it was the very next year—701 B.C.— that the Assyrians invaded the land. Hezekiah had fourteen more years to live and he certainly didn't want to do it in captivity. However, the Prophet Isaiah had already told him that God would deliver Judah and defend Jerusalem for the sake of King David (20:6), so Hezekiah had a great promise to believe. God's people don't live on explanations; they live on promises.

The Assyrian army chose Lachish for their central camp, thirty miles southwest of Jerusalem, and brought "a great host" against Jerusalem. Three of the Assyrian officers told Hezekiah to send out three of his officers to arrange for the terms of surrender.

These are titles and not personal names: Tartan = supreme commander, Rabsaris = chief officer, and Rabshakeh = field commander. Representing Hezekiah were Eliakim, the palace administrator, Shebna, the secretary, and Joah, the recorder (see Isa. 22:15-25; 36:3).

They met at the very place where Isaiah had confronted Ahaz, Hezekiah's father, and told him not to make a treaty with the Assyrians (Isa. 7; 2 Kings 16:5-9). Treaty or no treaty, Isaiah had predicted that the Assyrians would return, and his words had now come true.

The six officers didn't have a quiet conversation but stood far enough apart that the field commander had to raise his voice. Of course, the Assyrians wanted the people on the wall to hear what was going on, because they wanted to frighten them. The officers refused to speak in Aramaic, the trade language of that day, but used the familiar Hebrew (18:26-27; 32:18; 36:11-12). It's significant that the Assyrian leaders learned the Hebrew language so they could better wage war. God's servants today need to follow this example so they can proclaim the message of peace.

The proclamation (18:19-36; 32:9-19; 36:4-21). It's important to identify three "speeches" if we want to understand the dynamics of this event. First, the field commander spoke to Hezekiah and the Jews and blasphemed their God (18:17-36). Then Hezekiah went to the temple and spoke to God about what the field commander had said (19:1-19). Finally, God spoke to Hezekiah (through Isaiah the Prophet) about the judgment the Assyrians would receive at His hand (19:20-34). God always has the last word.

The field commander was a subtle man who knew how to weave words together and get his message across. Of course, he wasn't too concerned about speaking the truth, for he knew that most people (including the Jews in Jerusalem) live on "seems" instead of "is" and think with their emotions instead of their minds. The basic theme of his address was *faith* (18:19-20; 32:10; 36:4-5), and he asked the people, "What are you really trusting? Can anybody deliver you?" Note the repetition of the words "deliver" and "my hand," and not also how he tried to belittle Hezekiah by calling Sennacherib "the great king" (18:19, 28; Isa. 36:4, 13). What the Rabshekah didn't realize was that Jehovah is the Great King and that He heard every word the Field Commander was saying. "For the Lord Most High is awesome; He is a great King over all the earth" (Ps. 47:2, NKJV). Jerusalem was "the city of the great King" (Ps. 48:2), and the Lord Himself has said, "I am a great King" (Mal. 1:14, NKJV).

The Field Commander began to name what Judah was trusting, all the while pointing out that each of them would fail. He began with Egypt (18:21, 24; Isa. 36:6, 9), and no doubt there were officials in Judah who thought Pharaoh could help them. There had always been a strong Egyptian party in Judah after the kingdom divided, and the Prophet Isaiah had warned the leaders not to go to Egypt for help (Isa. 30:1-7; 31:1-3). But Egypt was nothing but a "splintered reed" that would pierce your hand if you leaned on it.[2]

In 18:22 and 30 (32:12; Isa. 36:7, 10), the commander tried to convince them that they couldn't trust the Lord their God to deliver them. How could they trust Jehovah when Hezekiah had removed the altars of the Lord from the city? Was the Lord pleased with what the king did? The Commander knew that there were people in Jerusalem who were unhappy because they could no longer worship at different altars and in the high places but had to go to the temple. But the Commander was so bold as to affirm that he and the Assyrian army had come to Jerusalem in obedience to the commandment of the Lord (18:25; 36:10; see 2 Chron. 35:21). After all, the Lord had used Assyria to chasten and destroy the kingdom of Israel, so why wouldn't He use Assyria to conquer Judah?

If the people of Judah were trusting in their military resources, said the commander, they were really in trouble, for they didn't have sufficient horses or enough cavalry men to put on them. If the king would "make a bargain" (enter into a treaty) with Sennacherib, the Assyrians would stop the siege and the people's lives would be spared.

In reply to the interruption by Eliakim, Shebna, and Joah (18:26), the field commander gave a special message to the people on the wall. If they didn't surrender, the day would come when they would be so hungry and thirsty that they would eat and drink their own excrement (18:27; 36:12). The report in 2 Chronicles 32:11 states that the field commander began his speech by warning the people of inevitable death by famine and thirst if they refused to surrender.

But the year before, the Prophet Isaiah had told Hezekiah that God would defend Jerusalem and destroy the Assyrians (20:6; Isa. 38:4-6), and it was this promise that the king gave to the people (18:29-30). Once again, we marvel at how much the commander knew about the affairs of Hezekiah. The commander was doing everything he could to tear down the people's confidence in their king. The Rabshakeh painted a glowing picture what would happen if Judah surrendered. They would live at peace in their own land until they would be deported to Assyria, a land very much like Judah (18:31-32; 36:16-17). Whenever the enemy makes an offer, there is always that fatal "until" attached to it.

The commander's final argument was purely pragmatic and very illogical: none of the gods of the nations already conquered could defeat Sennacherib, so Jehovah would fail as well (18:33-35; 36:18-20). But Jehovah isn't like the dead powerless idols of the nations: He is the true and living God! In obedience to the king's command, the people on the wall said nothing to the field commander, and that's the best way to respond to ignorant people who blaspheme the Lord and know nothing of His truth and greatness.

The humiliation (18:37–19:13; 36:22–37:13) The three officials left the fuller's field and returned to the city to tell Hezekiah what the field commander had said. In humility before the Lord and in acknowledgement of their own helplessness, the three men tore their garments and looked to the Lord for His help. Their told their king what the field commander had said, and the report must have broken Hezekiah's heart. How could anybody be so arrogant and so blaspheme the name of the Lord? The

Rabshakeh had reproached the living God by daring to associate Him with the dead idols of the nations. Hezekiah also tore his clothes and humbled himself before the Lord.

The king knew that he needed a word from the Lord, so he sent his officers to Isaiah the Prophet and asked him to pray and seek God's help. (This is the first mention of Isaiah in 2 Kings.) The king's metaphor about birth is a picture of extreme danger. The child has come to the time of birth, but the mother hasn't strength enough to deliver it, so both mother and child are in danger of losing their lives. The king also knew that only a remnant of God's people from Israel and Judah were faithful to Him (19:4, 30), but for their sake and the sake of David, the Lord would be willing to work.

Isaiah told Hezekiah not to be afraid (Ps. 46:1-3) because the Lord had heard the blasphemy of the Rabshakeh and would deal with Sennacherib. The Assyrian king would hear a report and the Lord would give him such a fearful spirit that he would return home. The report was that Tirhakah, king of Egypt,[3] was coming to Judah, which meant Sennacherib would have to wage war on two fronts (19:9; 37:9). He didn't want to do that, so he temporarily abandoned the siege and went back to Lachish to prepare for war. However the field commander sent one last message to Hezekiah, this time a letter (19:8-13; 37:8-13) and simply repeated what he had already said

Hezekiah the intercessor (2 Kings 19:14-19; 2 Chron. 32:20; Isa. 37:14-20)
When the outlook is bleak, try the uplook. That's what King Hezekiah did when he received the blasphemous letter from the king of Assyria. Often in my own ministry I have had to spread letters before the Lord and trust Him to work matters out, and He always has.

Hezekiah looked beyond his own throne and the throne of the "great king" Sennacherib and focused his attention on the throne of God "who was enthroned between the cherubim" (19:15; 37:14, NIV; see Pss. 80:1; 99:1). Since he was not a high priest, Hezekiah couldn't enter the Holy of Holies where the mercy seat sat upon the ark of the covenant, but he could "enter" by faith even as believers can today (Heb. 10:19-25). At each end of the mercy seat was a cherub, and the mercy seat was the throne of God on earth (Ex. 25:10-22). Not only is the Lord the King of Israel and the King of all nations, but He is the creator of the heavens and the earth. Hezekiah was lost in worship as he realized the greatness of the Lord, the only true God. This is a good example to follow when we pray about life's problems. When we focus on the Lord and see how great He is, it helps to put our problems in perspective,

The king had one great burden on his heart: that the God of Israel be glorified before the nations of the earth. Sennacherib had blasphemed the Lord and Hezekiah asked God to act on behalf of Judah so that His name would be honored. "Hallowed be thy name" is the first request in the Lord's Prayer (Matt. 6:9). Being a faithful Jew, the king knew that the gods of the defeated nations weren't gods at all (Isa. 2:20; 40:19-20; 41:7; 44:9-20). He asked the Lord to save the people of Judah, not for their sake but for the glory of His great name.[4]

Some people rush into the Lord's presence whenever they face a problem, but the Lord never hears their voices at any other time. This wasn't true of King Hezekiah. He was a man who at all times sought the blessing of the Lord on His people. He sought to know the Word of God and the will of God, and this gave him power in prayer. Blessed is that nation whose leaders know how to pray!

Hezekiah the victor (2 Kings 19:20-37; 2 Chron. 32:20-22; Isa. 37:21-38)

The Lord told Isaiah to get His message to the king, and the prophet obeyed. The answer to Hezekiah's prayer was threefold: (1) God would deliver Jerusalem, (2) God would defeat the Assyrian army and they would depart, and (3) God would care for the people and they would not starve. But God also had a message of rebuke to Sennacherib because of his pride and blasphemy. Hezekiah's faith was rewarded and his prayer was answered.

Rebuke (19:20-28; 37:22-29). God had used Assyria to chasten the northern kingdom of Israel, and the Lord had given Sennacherib victory over other nations, but the Assyrian king had never given God the glory. In fact, his field commander had reproached the name of the Lord (19:4, 16, 22, 24; 37:4, 17, 23, 24) and blasphemed the God of Israel. But "the virgin, the daughter of Zion"—the city of Jerusalem—would toss her head in disdain and laugh at the defeat of Assyria. The Lord used the image of a virgin because the Assyrians would not be able to take the city and violate it the way pagan soldiers did to women taken captive. But the Lord would treat the Assyrians like cattle and put hooks in their noses and lead them.

The Lord quoted back to the Rabshakeh and to Sennacherib the very words they had used in boasting about their victories. Chariots are made primarily for the flat lands, but they boasted that their chariots had ascended the high mountains of Lebanon. The dry lands and deserts didn't stop them, nor did the rivers. Other kings used barges to cross rivers, but they dried up the Nile and walked across on dry land. (Is this a reference to Israel at the Jordan, Joshua 4–5? There is no evidence that Assyria ever conquered Egypt.) They cut down cities and people the way a farmer mows the grass, and nothing stood in their way.

But it was the Lord who planned these conquests and enabled Assyria to succeed (37:26-27). The nation was His weapon to judge Israel and the other nations and to chasten Judah. (Isa. 10:5-19). How foolish for the ax to boast against the woodsman, and how foolish for Sennacherib to take credit for what the Lord had done! Instead of honoring the Lord, Sennacherib raged against the Lord (19:27; 37:28-29) and exalted himself against the God of heaven. Whatever reasons or excuses world leaders may give for what they do, the basic cause is rebellion against God and His law (Ps. 2:1-6; Acts 4:23-31). But the Lord would treat the Assyrians like cattle, put hooks in their noses, and lead them away! The Assyrians were known for doing this to their prisoners of war, but now they would be the victims.

Provision (19:29; 37:30). The Assyrians had taken possession of Judah, pillaged the land and taken the fortified cities, and now they were besieging Jerusalem. How long could the food hold out? And even if Jerusalem did survive, how long would it take to restore the land, plant the crops, and get a harvest? The field commander warned that the people of Jerusalem would die of famine and thirst if they didn't submit to Assyria (2 Chron. 32:11). But the Lord of the harvest was in control. September and October were the months devoted to sowing, and March and April were devoted to reaping the harvest. The orchards and vineyards produced their harvest from July to September. No doubt the Assyrians came in the harvest season and confiscated the food. With the Assyrians in the land and Jerusalem under siege, the people couldn't work their farms; but God promised that when the Assyrians left, food would grow of itself until the men could work the fields, orchards, and vineyards. God would not permit His people to starve.

Some students have seen a relationship between this prophecy and Psalm 126, one of the "Songs of the ascents [degrees]." (See chapter 10, endnote 3.) The psalm speaks of a dramatic and sudden deliverance for Jerusalem, which certainly wasn't the case at the end of the Babylonian captivity. Could this have been Jerusalem's deliverance from the Assyrian army, when God killed 185,000 soldiers? If so, the prayer in Psalm 126:4 would certainly be applicable. As the men went out in the fields to sow, they would be weeping for joy that the land was delivered, but they might also weep because the seed they were sowing could have been made into bread for their children. Seed was scarce, yet God cared for His people.

Deliverance (19:28, 30-37; 32:21-22; 37:31-38). God promised that He would deliver His "remnant" from their enemies and they would "take root" and become fruitful again. Not only would Sennacherib never enter the city, but he wouldn't even shoot an arrow at it, attack it, or build a siege mound next to it! In one night, God's angel killed 185,000 Assyrian soldiers and that put an end to the siege of Jerusalem. The Rabshakeh had boasted that one of the Assyrian junior officers was stronger than 2,000 Jewish charioteers (36:8-9), but when the Lord wanted to wipe out 185,000 enemy soldiers, all He had to do was send one of His angels!

It was a humiliating defeat for the Assyrians, but the event brought great glory to the Lord and honor to Hezekiah (2 Chron. 32:23; see Ps. 126:2-3). Sennacherib left the scene and went home, and there one of his sons killed him. His gods were unable to give him victory in Judah and they couldn't protect him from his own family in his own homeland. Why did God deliver His people? For the glory of His own name, of course, and for the sake of David whom He loved (19:34). Why does He bless His people today? For the sake of His own glory and because of His love for His own Son who died for us.

Death (2 Kings 20:20-21; 2 Chron. 32:27-33). "And Hezekiah prospered in all that he did," states 2 Chronicles 32:30 (NASB). Because of the blessing of the Lord, he had immense wealth, huge flocks and herds, and large storage buildings for grain and win. "He trusted in the Lord, the God of Israel" (2 Kings 18:5, NASB). "And the Lord was with him; wherever he went he prospered" (2 Kings 18:7, NASB). He was a model of the "blessed man" in Psalm 1., the person who obeys the Word, meditates on it, and depends upon the power of God.

Hezekiah was not only in favor with God, but he was also beloved by his people. He was buried with the kings in Jerusalem, "and all Judah and the inhabitants of Jerusalem honored him at his death" (2 Chron. 32:33). Like all of us, Hezekiah had his lapses of faith and his failures, but was undoubtedly one of the greatest kings in Jewish history.

TWELVE

2 KINGS 21:1–23:30
[2 CHRONICLES 33:1–35:27]

The End Is Near

We live in the twilight of a great civilization, amid the deepening decline of modern culture," writes eminent theologian Carl F. H. Henry. "Those strange beast-empires of the books of Daniel and Revelation seem already to be stalking and sprawling over the surface of the earth."[1]

Similar words could have been written about Judah during the days of the three kings studied in this chapter—Manasseh, Amon, and Josiah. The Jewish nation had given the world a witness to the one true and living God, but now many of the people worshiped foreign idols. Israel gave the world the prophets and the Scriptures, but most of the leaders of Judah no longer listened to God's Word. Josiah was Judah's last good king. The Lord had covenanted to protect David's throne so that the promised Redeemer might one day come, but now the government of Judah was decaying and the very existence of the kingdom was in jeopardy. The future of God's plan of redemption for a lost world rested with the faithful remnant that resisted the inroads of pagan culture and remained true to the Lord.

God's promise hadn't changed: "If my people, which are called by my name, shall humble themselves, and pray, and seek my

147

face, and turn from their wicked ways; then will I hear from heaven, and will forgive their sin, and will heal their land" (2 Chron. 7:14). Each of these three kings had to learn something about humility. It was almost too late when Manasseh humbled himself (2 Chron. 33:12, 19); Amon never did submit to the Lord (33:23); and Josiah truly humbled himself before the Lord and was used to bring a spiritual awakening to the land (34:19, 27). "True humility is a healthy thing," wrote A. W. Tozer. "The humble man accepts the truth about himself."[2]

Manasseh—humiliated by affliction (2 Kings 21:1-18; 2 Chron. 33:1-20)
That godly King Hezekiah should have such a wicked son is another one of those puzzles in biblical history. If Manasseh was born in 709, then he was seven years old when his father was healed and the miracle of the shadow occurred. He was eight years old when the 185,000 Assyrian soldiers were slain. Apparently these miracles made little impression on his heart. Many scholars think that Manasseh was coregent with his father for perhaps ten years (697–687), from ages twelve to twenty-two, and the son lived in close relationship with a godly father.[3] But the remarkable thing is that Manasseh became the most wicked king in Judah's history, so much so that he is blamed for the fall of the Southern Kingdom (2 Kings 24:3; Jer. 15:1-4).

Manasseh's wickedness (23:1-15; 33:1-10). He lived a most ungodly life and yet had the longest reign of any king in Jewish history. It was as though the Lord took His hand off the nation and allowed all the filth to pour out of people's hearts. In character and conduct, he was even worse than the Amorites whom Joshua defeated in Canaan, a nation with a reputation for brutality and wickedness (21:11; Gen. 15:16). All that his godly father Hezekiah had torn down, Manasseh rebuilt as he led the nation back into idolatry, including the worship of Baal. He also made a detestable idol which he placed in the temple of the Lord (21:3; 2 Chron. 33:7, 15), and he encouraged the people to worship "all the starry hosts" (21:3; 33:3, 5; see Deut. 4:19 and 17:1-7).

There was to be but one altar in the temple court, but Manasseh added altars dedicated to various gods (see 16:10-16) and thus made Jehovah one "god" among many. Yet the Lord had put His name in only one place—the temple in Jerusalem (21:4, 7; Deut. 12:11; 1 Kings 8:20, 29; 9:3); and now a multitude of false gods shared that honor with Him. Manasseh followed the religion of Molech and caused his sons to pass through the altar fire (Lev. 18:21; 20:1-5), and he consulted spiritists and mediums (21:6; 33:6; Lev. 19:31; Deut. 18:11).

In His mercy, the Lord sent prophets to warn the king and the people, but they refused to listen. Some of these witnesses were no doubt killed by the king (21:16), along with other godly people who opposed the worship of false gods. God reminded His people that their enjoyment of the land depended on their obedience to the law of the Lord. This was the basic requirement of the covenant God made with His people (Lev. 26; Deut. 28–29). God had promised to keep them in the Promised Land (2 Sam. 7:10), but now He warned them that they would be taken off the land and scattered among the nations (Deut. 28:64-68; Lev. 26:33-35). This judgment had already fallen on the Northern Kingdom with the invasion of the Assyrian army, and it would happen to Judah when the Babylonians came (606–586). Alas, Judah didn't learn from Israel's chastening.

We don't know which prophets delivered the message in 21:10-15, but nobody could misunderstand what they said. If Manasseh and the people didn't repent and turn from their evil ways, God would send judgment so severe that just hearing about it would make their ears tingle (21:12; 1 Sam. 3:11; Jer. 19:3). This describes a frightening response to news so terrible that it's like hearing a loud noise that makes your ears ring. The Hebrew word *salal* means "to tingle, to quiver," and is related to the word for cymbals and bells. When they heard the news of the approaching Babylonian army, it would be like hearing a sudden clash of cymbals! Wake up! Wake up! But it would be too late.

But God used a second image to awaken them. Like a careful builder, He would measure the nation with His plumbline, but it would be a measuring for tearing down and not for building up. Everyone was familiar with bricklayers using plumblines to keep the walls straight as they built, but nobody measures a building in order to destroy it. (See Isa. 34:11 and Amos 7:7-9, 17.) God's judgments are just and He will give them what they deserve, just as He gave Israel (Samaria) what she deserved. The third picture comes from the kitchen: God would empty the kingdom of Judah of its people just as a person wipes all the water out of a dish after washing it. It's the image of depopulating a land by death or deportation and leaving it empty (Jer. 51:34).

The word "forsake" in 21:14 means "to give over to judgment." God promised never to abandon His people (1 Sam. 12:22; 2 Sam. 7:23-24), but He also warned that He would chasten them if they disobeyed Him. God didn't break His promises; it was the people who broke His covenant. God is always faithful to His covenant, whether to bless obedience or punish disobedience.

Manasseh's repentance (33:11-13, 19). The writer of 2 Kings wrote nothing about the remarkable change in Manasseh's life, but we find the record in 2 Chronicles.[4] Apparently he displeased the king of Assyria in some way and God allowed the Assyrian officers to come to Judah and capture the king. This was no respectable act of taking somebody into custody, because they put a hook in his nose and bound him with chains (33:11, NIV). He was treated like a steer being led to the slaughter, and he deserved it. The city of Babylon was a second capital for Assyria at that time, and there they imprisoned him.

The whole experience was one of great humiliation for this wicked king, but the Lord used it to chasten him, break his pride, and bring him to his knees. He prayed to the Lord for forgiveness and the Lord kept His promise and forgave him (2 Chron. 7:14). Even more, the Lord moved the Assyrians to set him free and allow him to return to Jerusalem to rule over the people. What a trophy of the grace of God! Manasseh humbled himself (33:12), but the Lord first humbled him (33:19). True repentance is a work of God in the heart and a willing response of the heart to the Lord.

Manasseh's reformation (33:14-18, 20). When he returned home, Manasseh proved the reality of his conversion by seeking to undo all the evil he had done. He fortified Jerusalem and other cities in Judah, he removed his idol from the temple (33:7, 15), and he removed from the temple all the altars he had put up to false gods. Having purged the temple, he then repaired the altar of the Lord that had been neglected, and he offered thank offerings to the Lord who had rescued him. He commanded the people of Judah to serve the Lord and he set the example. He allowed them to offer sacrifices in the high places, but not to pagan gods—only to the God of Israel. "Therefore bear fruit in keeping with repentance," John the Baptist told the Pharisees and Sadducees (Matt. 3:8, NASB), and that's exactly what Manasseh did.

After a long life and reign, Manasseh died and was buried in the garden at his own house, not in the sepulchers of the kings (see 28:27).

Amon—hardened by disobedience (2 Kings 21:19-26; 2 Chron. 33:21-25)
After his repentance, Manasseh tried to undo all the damage he had done to Jerusalem and Judah, but there was one place where he could make no changes—in the heart of his son Amon. The young man had been too influenced by his father's sins to take notice of his new life of obedience, and there were no doubt people at court who encouraged Amon to maintain the old ways. Whereas Manasseh humbled himself before the Lord, his son Amon refused to do so (33:23), and the longer he sinned, the harder his heart became.

"The wages of sin is death" (Rom. 6:23). Why Amon's own officials should assassinate him isn't made clear, but the reason probably wasn't spiritual. While it's true that the Law of Moses declared that idolaters should be slain (Deut. 13), there was nobody in the land with the authority to deal with an idolatrous king. It's likely that the conspirators were more interested in politics. Amon was probably pro-Assyrian—after all, they had released his father from prison—while the officials were pro-Babylonian, not realizing that the rise of Babylon would ultimately mean the fall of Judah. Amon's son Josiah was definitely pro-Babylonian and even lost his life on the battlefield trying to stop the Egyptian army from assisting Assyria against Babylon. The fact that the people made Josiah the next king would suggest that they didn't want a pro-Assyria king.

Josiah—humbled by God's Word (2 Kings 22:1–23:30; 2 Chron. 34:1–35:25)
Out of the twenty rulers of Judah, including wicked Queen Athaliah, only eight of them could be called "good": Asa, Jehoshaphat, Joash, Amaziah, Uzziah, Jotham, Hezekiah and Josiah. There's no question that Josiah was a great king, for even the Prophet Jeremiah used him as an example for the other rulers to follow. "He pled the cause of the afflicted and needy," said Jeremiah of Josiah, while the kings that followed Josiah exploited the people so they could build their elaborate palaces (Jer. 22:11-17). Josiah ruled for thirty-one years (640–609) and walked in the ways of the Lord because David was his model. No doubt his mother was a godly woman and guided her son wisely. He was only eight years old when they made him king, so the court officials were his mentors; but at age sixteen, Josiah committed himself to the Lord and began to seek His blessing.

Cleansing the land (34:3-7). Hezekiah had cleaned up after Ahaz, and Manasseh had cleansed up the consequences of his own evil practices, and now twenty-year-old Josiah had to undo the damage done by his father Amon. What a tragedy that all the leaders of Judah didn't maintain the law of the Lord and keep the nation honoring Jehovah. The four kings who followed Josiah undid all the good he had done and sold the nation into the hands of the Babylonians. Everything rises and falls with leadership, and young King Josiah provided aggressive spiritual leadership for the people. He had been seeking the Lord for four years and now he was prepared to cleanse the land.

He purged the land of the high places and called the people back to worship at the temple in Jerusalem. He destroyed the idols and the altars dedicated to Baal and other false gods, and he defiled the places where the people worshiped these idols. After purging Jerusalem and Judah, he moved into northern Israel (Manasseh, Ephraim, Naphtali) and rid that area of idolatry. It's interesting that the king of Judah could go to these tribes in Israel (Samaria) and exercise such authority, but a great many people had come to Hezekiah's Passover feast from Ephraim, Manasseh, Issachar, and Zebulun and returned home determined to please the Lord (2 Chron. 30:18). From 2 Chronicles 34:7, we learn that the king personally went on these trips and led the way in removing idolatry from the land.[5]

Repairing the temple (22:3-7; 34:8-13). Josiah's eighteenth year as king was indeed a stellar one. He repaired the temple of the Lord where the Book of the Law was discovered; he made a covenant with the Lord; he carried on further reforms in the land, and he hosted a great celebration of Passover. He was twenty-six at the time. The man who expedited the king's plans for repairing the temple was Shaphan, the father of a remarkable family. His son Gemariah joined with others in urging King Jehoiakim not to burn Jeremiah's scroll, and his grandson Micaiah heard Baruch read Jeremiah's second scroll in the temple and reported it to the king's secretaries (Jer. 36:11ff). His son Elasah carried Jeremiah's letter to the Jewish exiles in Babylon (Jer. 29:1-23), and his son Ahikam was among the men who consulted Huldah the Prophetess about the Book of the Law (1 Kings 22:12-20). Ahikam also interceded with King Jehoiakim not to kill the Prophet Jeremiah (Jer. 26:16-24). After the fall of Judah and Jerusalem, Shaphan's grandson Gadaliah was named governor of Judah. The only disappointing son of the four was Jaazaniah who worshiped idols in the temple of the Lord (Ezek. 8:11-12).

The people had been contributing money for the upkeep of the temple (v. 4), so the king ordered Shaphan to tell Hilkiah the high priest to distribute the funds to the workers and start repairing the temple. It wasn't enough just to destroy the idol worship in the land; the temple had to be available for the worship of the true and living God. As with the temple reconstruction under Joash (2 Kings 12), the workers were faithful and there was no need to keep elaborate records. Leadership is stewardship, and leaders must see to it that the work is done with integrity and God's money be used wisely.

Discovering the Scriptures (22:8-20; 34:14-28). It seems remarkable that the Book of the Law should be lost *in the temple!* That would be like losing the Bible in a church building and not missing it for years. This scroll was probably all five books of Moses, but Shaphan "read in the book"; that is, he read the king-selected passages, perhaps from the Book of Deuteronomy.[6] Shaphan gave the king a report on the building program and then, almost as an afterthought, told him about the newly discovered book. It's to Josiah's credit that he desired to hear what the book said, and when he heard it read, he was smitten with fear and grief. How people respond to God's Word is a good indication of their spiritual appetite and the strength of their desire to please the Lord.

If indeed Shaphan read from the Book of Deuteronomy, then what Josiah heard read from chapters 4–13 would convict him about the wicked things the nation *had already done.* Chapters 14–18 would disturb him because of what the people *had not done,* and the covenant spelled out in chapters 27–30 would warn him of *what God would do* if the nation didn't repent. In the terms of His covenant, the Lord made it clear that the nation would be punished severely if they disobeyed His law. So deeply moved was the king that he tore his robes and ordered the high priest and several officers to inquire of the Lord concerning Judah's spiritual condition. Josiah was only twenty-six years old and had been seeking the Lord for only ten years, yet his response to the Word of God was that of a mature believer.

Hilkiah didn't consult Jeremiah about this matter, or even the Prophet Zephaniah, one of Josiah's kinsmen (Zeph. 1:1), who was ministering at that same time. Perhaps Jeremiah was not in the city but at his family home in Anathoth, and Zephaniah may also have been out of Jerusalem. But the king's committee found a capable servant in Huldah the Prophetess, whose husband Shallum was in charge of the royal wardrobe.[7] Along with Hulduh, the prophetesses in Scripture include Miriam (Ex. 15:20), Deborah (Jud. 4:4), Naodiah (Neh. 6:14), the wife of Isaiah the Prophet (Isa. 8:3), Anna (Luke 2:36), and the four daughters of Philip the evangelist (Acts 21:8-9).

Huldah's message was in two parts. The first part (22:15-17; 34:23-25) was addressed to "the man who sent you," meaning Josiah as a common man before the law of God, just like all the other people in Judah and Israel. The second part (22:18-20; 34:26-28) was addressed to "the king of Judah," that is, Josiah as an individual with spiritual needs and concerns. As far as the nation was concerned, God would indeed send His wrath because of their repeated disobedience, but as far as Josiah was concerned, he would be spared this impending judgment because of his godly life and humility before the Lord (see 2 Chron. 33:12, 23). Even though Josiah died as the result of wounds received in battle, he went to his grave in peace because Nebuchadnezzar and his army hadn't yet invaded the land. God called Josiah away before the terrible judgments fell.

Covenanting with the Lord (23:1-3; 34:29-33). The delegation reported Huldah's message to the king, who immediately called the elders, priests, and prophets together, with the people of the land, and shared the message with them. Then he called them to enter with him into a covenant with the Lord. The "renewing of the covenant" was a familiar event in Jewish history. When the new generation was about to enter Canaan, Moses had them renew the covenant, as recorded in Deuteronomy. On two occasions, Joshua called for a renewal of the covenant (Josh. 8:34ff; 24), and so also did Samuel (1 Sam. 7:2ff; 12:1ff). After Nehemiah and the people completed the rebuilding of the wall of Jerusalem, Ezra led them to rededicate themselves to Jehovah (Neh. 8–10). We must never assume today that because our churches are growing and our ministry prospering that God's people are necessarily at their best. There are times when corporate renewal of our dedication to Christ is the right thing to do.

The king stood by a pillar of the temple (see 11:14) and read the words of the law to the assembly. He covenanted with them to walk before the Lord in obedience and devotion. He set the example, for if the leaders don't walk with God, how can God give His people His best blessings? This meeting wasn't a demonstration of "civil religion" where everybody obeyed because the king commanded it. What Josiah pled for was a yielding of their hearts and souls to the Lord in sincerity and truth.

Reforming the land (23:4-20; 34:33). The king then began to implement the terms of the covenant and obey the law of the Lord. First, he removed from the temple everything that belonged to idolatrous worship, burned it in the Kidron Valley and had the ashes taken to Bethel and scattered to defile the shrine of the golden calf that Jeroboam I had set up. He also broke down that shrine and destroyed everything associated with it (23:15; Hos. 10:5; Zeph. 1:4). He brought Manasseh's infamous idol out of the temple (see 21:7; 33:7), burned and pulverized it, and sprinkled the ashes on the graves of those who worshiped it so as to defile them. Josiah destroyed the houses of the sodomites (male religious prostitutes; 1 Kings 14:24 and 15:12), in obedience to Deuteronomy 23:17-18.

He also removed the Levitical priests who ministered at the high places throughout Judah (23:8), from the northern border (Geba) to the southern border (Beersheba), desecrated those places, and brought the priests to Jerusalem. They were not permitted to serve at the temple altar, but they were allowed to share the food from the sacrifices. Then he went to Topheth, the place of human sacrifice in the Valley of Hinnom, and defiled it. (See Isa. 30:33, Jer. 7:31-32, and 19:6, 11-14.) He removed the horses dedicated to the sun god and burned the chariots in the fire. Imagine stabling horses in the temple precincts! He pulled down and destroyed the altars to the heavenly host that had been placed by Ahaz on the roof of the temple buildings (16:1-4, 10-16; 21:3, 21-22), removed by Hezekiah and replaced by Manasseh. (See Jer.

19:13 and 32:29.) He also did away with the altars Manasseh had put in the temple court. All these things were smashed and thrown in the garbage dump in the Kidron Valley.

On the southern slope of the Mount of Olives, Solomon had provided special altars for his heathen wives where they could worship their gods (1 Kings 11:5-7), and these altars and idols Josiah removed and destroyed. To make sure the area would never be used for idol worship again, he buried human bones there and defiled it (Num. 19:16). He even took his crusade into Samaria and destroyed the shrine at Bethel that had been established by King Jeroboam (1 Kings 12:28-33). He took the remains of the dead priests of Bethel, buried nearby, and burned them on the altar, scattering the ashes to pollute the area. Thus he fulfilled the prophecy made three centuries before (1 Kings 13:31-32). When Josiah saw the grave of the man of God who had prophesied those very actions, he commanded that it be left intact.

What Josiah did at Bethel, he did throughout the land of Samaria, destroying idols and the shrines dedicated to them, and slaying the idolatrous priests who served at their altars (Deut. 13:6-11; 18:20). Don't confuse the idolatrous priests of verse 20 with the disobedient priests of verse 8. The latter were allowed to live in Jerusalem but were not permitted to serve at that temple altar. Finally, Josiah removed the various kinds of spirit mediums from the land (23:24), people who were at one time encouraged by King Manasseh (21:6). But in spite of all the good that Josiah did, he couldn't stop the Lord from sending judgment to Judah. The sins of Manasseh had been so great that nothing could prevent the Lord from pouring out His wrath on His people.

Celebrating the Passover (23:21-23; 35:1-19). In many respects, King Josiah was following the example of King Hezekiah in cleansing the nation of idolatry, repairing the temple and restoring the worship, and celebrating a great nationwide Passover in Jerusalem. While all the appointed feasts in Leviticus 23 were meaningful and important, the feast of Passover was especially significant. For one thing, Passover reminded the Jewish people of their national origin at the Exodus when the Lord delivered them from Egyptian bondage. This was a manifestation of the grace and power of God. He took them to Himself as His own people and entered into a covenant relationship with them at Mount Sinai. They were God's chosen people, God's covenant people, a people to bring glory to His name.

Hezekiah had celebrated his great Passover during the second month of the year, but Josiah celebrated during the first month. Note in 2 Chronicles 35 that there is an emphasis on the Levites and their important ministry during the Passover (vv. 2, 5, 8-12, 14-15, 18). According to 2 Kings 23:22 and 2 Chronicles 35:18, this Passover was even greater than the one celebrated in Hezekiah's time because "all Judah and Israel . . . were present" (35:18; see 30:18). Hezekiah's Passover lasted two weeks, but at Josiah's Passover the people offered almost twice as many sacrifices. At least 37,600 small animals were offered, plus 3,800 bulls. The priests and Levites were cleansed and sanctified, ready to serve, and there were many Levites who sang praises to the Lord and played instruments.

Josiah obeyed what he had read in the law of the Lord.

What is the meaning of King Josiah's admonition to the Levites about carrying the ark (35:3)? Bearing the sacred ark had been the task of the Kohathites (Num. 4), but the nation was no longer a pilgrim people and the ark had been placed in the Holy of Holies in the temple. Inasmuch as the Book of the Law had been misplaced, and it was kept in the ark (Deut. 31:24-29), it has been conjectured that perhaps the ark had been taken out of the temple and hidden during the evil days of Manasseh and the ark and the book were separated. It's also been suggested that Manasseh replaced the ark with the image he had made and which he worshiped (23:4-6; 33:7). The Hebrew word translated "put" in 35:3 can be translated "leave," so the sense of his command might be, "Don't bring the ark—we don't need it at this time. We're no longer on the march." Some of the enthusiastic Levites might have wanted to add the presence of the ark to the great celebration, even though the law didn't require it.

Josiah ruled at a time when Assyria was on the decline and Babylon hadn't yet reached its zenith, the times were more peaceful, and the people could travel in greater safety. The celebration was indeed a great rallying time for the Jewish people from both Judah and Samaria. God's people need occasions like this when together they can celebrate the Lord and His goodness and fellowship with one another.

Sacrificing his life (23:28-30; 35:20-27). Nineveh, the capital city of Assyria, was taken by the Babylonians and the Medes in 612 B.C., and Assyria was definitely on the decline. In 608, Pharaoh Neco led his army from Egypt to assist the Assyrians against the Babylonians.[8] Josiah was pro-Babylon and wasn't too happy about the Egyptian forces marching along the western border of Judah, so he personally led the army of Judah against him. The two armies met at Megiddo, about fifty miles north of Jerusalem, and there Josiah was fatally wounded. His officers took him back to Jerusalem where he died and was buried with the kings.

Josiah had no mandate from the Lord to interfere in the dispute between Egypt and Babylon, yet Pharaoh Neco claimed that the Lord had commanded him to help Assyria. According to 2 Chronicles 35:22, this message was "from the mouth of God." Egypt and Assyria failed in their attempt to hold back Babylon, but Neco's defeat of Josiah did give Egypt control of Judah for a few years (2 Chron. 36:3-4). Josiah was greatly mourned in Judah and Jeremiah even wrote laments to honor him (35:25; see Jer. 22:10). These laments have been lost and must not be confused with the Book of Lamentations.

From the death of Josiah in 608 to the destruction of Jerusalem by Babylon in 586—a period of twenty-two years—four different kings sat on David's throne, three of them sons of Josiah but not imitators of his faith. Jehoahaz and Jehoiachin each reigned for only three months. It was a sad time for the people of God, but there was still a believing remnant that followed the Lord and helped seekers in each new generation to know the Lord.

THIRTEEN

2 KINGS 23:29–25:30
[2 CHRONICLES 36]

The End Has Come

"Every great nation fell by suicide." The British political leader Richard Cobden made that observation, and his statement is aptly illustrated in the history of the kingdom of Judah. Sudden political or military blows from the outside didn't destroy Judah. The nation committed suicide as it decayed morally and spiritually from within. These chapters tell the tragic story of the last years of a great nation. We can see the steps in their decline and the decisions of their kings who led the people downward to destruction.

They lost their independence (2 Kings 23:29-33; 2 Chron. 35:20–36:1-4)
King Josiah was a godly man who sincerely wanted to serve the Lord, but he made a foolish blunder by attacking Pharaoh Neco. His meddling in Egypt's affairs was a personal political decision and not a command from the Lord. Josiah wanted to prevent Pharaoh Neco from assisting Assyria in their fight against Babylon, little realizing that it was Babylon and not Assyria that would be Judah's greatest enemy. Josiah was mortally wounded by an arrow at Megiddo and died in Jerusalem. With the death of

Josiah, the kingdom of Judah lost her independence and became subject to Egypt. This lasted from 609 to about 606, and then Egypt retreated and Babylon took over.

According to 1 Chronicles 3:15-16, Josiah had four sons: Johanan; Eliakim, who was renamed Jehoiakim; Mattaniah, who was renamed Zedekiah; and Shallum, also known as Jehoahaz. We know nothing about Johanan and assume he died in childhood. When Josiah died, the people put Josiah's youngest son Jehoahaz on the throne and bypassed the other two brothers. His given name was Shallum (Jer. 22:11) and Jehoahaz was the name he was given when he took the throne. Jehoahaz and Zedekiah were full brothers (23:31; 24:18). It's obvious that the Jeremiah mentioned in 23:31 isn't the Prophet Jeremiah since he was unmarried (Jer. 16:1-2).

Jehoahaz reigned only three months. When Neco was returning to Egypt with his army, he deposed Jehoahaz, made Eliakim king, renaming him Jehoiakim, and placed a heavy tax on the land. It's likely that Jehoiakim was pro-Egypt in politics while Jehoahaz favored alliances with Babylon, as had his father Josiah. Pharaoh met Jehoahaz at the Egyptian military headquarters at Riblah and from there took him to Egypt where Jehoahaz died. The Prophet Jeremiah had predicted this event. He told the people not to mourn the death of Josiah, but rather to mourn the exile of his son and successor Shallum, for he would never see Judah again (Jer. 22:10-12). But unlike his godly father Josiah, Jehoahaz was an ungodly man and an evil king and deserved to be exiled.

Jehovah called Israel to be a "people dwelling alone, not reckoning itself among the nations" (Num. 23:9, NKJV). Their faith was to be in the Lord alone, not in the treaties or compromises worked out by clever diplomats. Israel was God's "special treasure . . . a kingdom of priests and a holy nation" (Ex. 19:5-6, NKJV; see Deut. 7:6-11). It was Solomon who moved Israel from its separated position into the arena of international politics. He married seven hundred wives (1 Kings 11:3), most of whom represented treaties with their fathers or brothers who were rulers and men of influence. These treaties brought wealth into the nation and kept warfare out, but in the end, both Solomon and Israel were drawn into the idolatry of the nations around them (1 Kings 11:1-13).

Had the Jewish people obeyed the Lord and kept His covenant, He would have put them at the head of the nations (Deut. 28:1-14), but their disobedience led to their defeat and dispersal among the nations of the earth. Unfortunately, the church has followed Israel's bad example and entangled itself with the world instead of keeping itself separated from the world (2 Tim. 2:4; James 1:27; 1 John 2:15-17). Believers are in the world but not of the world, and this enables us to go into the world and share Jesus Christ with lost sinners (John 17:13-19). Campbell Morgan said that the church did the most for the world when the church was the least like the world. Be distinct!

They lost their land (2 Kings 23:34–24:7; 2 Chron. 36:5-8)
Having deposed Jehoahaz, Pharaoh Neco selected Josiah's second son to be the next regent, changing his name from Eliakim to Jehoiakim. Both names mean "God has established," but the new name used the covenant name "Jehovah" in place of "El," the common name for God. By doing this, Neco was claiming to be the Lord's agent in ruling Judah. Of course, the new king had to swear allegiance to Neco in the name of Jehovah, and his new name would remind him of his obligations. In order to pay tribute to Neco, the new king taxed the people of the land. He reigned for eleven years and during that time, Judah got more and more in trouble with the surrounding nations.

Jehoiakim was a wicked man. When Urijah the Prophet denounced him and then fled to Egypt, Jehoiakim sent his men to find him and kill him (Jer. 26:20-24). Jeremiah the Prophet announced that Jehoiakim would not be mourned when he died but would have the burial of a donkey, not the burial of a king (Jer. 22:18-19). It was Jehoiakim who cut to pieces and burned to ashes the scroll of Jeremiah's prophecy (Jer. 36). Unlike his father Josiah, he had no respect for the Lord or His Word (Jer. 22:1-23).

However, the new empire of Babylon was about to replace Egypt as Judah's great enemy and master. Nebuchadnezzar their king attacked Egypt, but the battle ended in a stalemate and Nebuchadnezzar returned to Babylon to reequip and strengthen his forces for a return engagement. From Babylon's "retreat," Jehoiakim falsely concluded that Egypt was strong enough to resist Babylon, so after three years as a vassal king, he rebelled against Nebuchadnezzar and refused to pay the annual tribute. Until he could arrive at Jerusalem in person, Nebuchadnezzar ordered the armies of some of his vassal nations to attack and raid Judah. These raids were but a prelude to the great invasion of Judah that would lead to the destruction of Jerusalem and the temple. Isaiah had told King Hezekiah that this would happen (2 Kings 20:12-20) and King Manasseh had heard the same warning but not heeded it (21:10-15). Jeremiah had seen the vision of the boiling pot that faced the north, symbolizing the coming invasion from Babylon (Jer. 1:11-16; see 4:5-9; 6:22-26).

The scenario of the death of King Jehoiakim must be put together from information given in 2 Kings, 2 Chronicles, and the Book of Jeremiah. In 597, Nebuchadnezzar came to Jerusalem to punish the rebellious king; but before he arrived, his officers had captured Jehoiakim and bound him to take him prisoner to Babylon (2 Chron. 36:5-6). We aren't told whether he died a natural death or was killed (2 Kings 24:6); the verse mentions only his death ("slept with his fathers") and not his burial. He died in December 598, before Nebuchadnezzar arrived on the scene in March 597 (2 Kings 24:10ff). The Prophet Jeremiah warned that Jehoiakim would have an ignominious death and no burial. When the king died, his body was probably thrown into some pit outside the walls of Jerusalem. He lived a disgraceful life and fittingly was buried in a disgraceful manner.

They lost their wealth and their leading people (2 Kings 24:8-17; 25:27-30; 36:9-10)
Nebuchadnezzar appointed Jehoiakim's son Jehoiachin (Jeconiah, Coniah) to be the new king, but he lasted only three

months. He was eighteen years old at the time.[1] When the Babylonian king, officials, and army arrived at Jerusalem in March, 597, Jehoiachin led the royal family and the leaders of the nation in surrendering to the enemy. Jeremiah had prophesied this humiliating event (Jer. 22:24-30). The Babylonians took the king's treasures as well as treasures from the temple of the Lord. Some of the temple vessels had already been removed to Babylon (2 Chron. 36:7), but now the Babylonians stripped off all the gold they could find. Then they deported to Babylon over ten thousand key people, including members of the royal family, government officials, and valuable craftsmen. This is when the Prophet Ezekiel was taken to Babylon (Ezek. 1:1-3). All of this was but a foretaste of the terrible events that would occur when Nebuchadnezzar would return in 588 and lay siege to Jerusalem for two years. (See Isa. 39:1-8, Jer. 7:1-15 and Ezek. 20:1-49.)

Jehoiachin was a prisoner in Babylon for thirty-seven years and then was released by Nebuchadnezzar's son and heir, Evil-Merodoch (2 Kings 25:27-30; Jer. 52:31-34). The false prophet Hananiah had predicted that Jehoiachin would be set free to return to Judah (Jer. 28), but the king remained an exile, though treated with kindness after his pardon. Whenever the king of Babylon displayed his special prisoners on royal occasions, he put Jehoiachin's throne above the thrones of the other captive kings. As Jeremiah had predicted, none of Jehoiachin's children sat on David's throne (Jer. 22:28-30), because Josiah's third son Mattaniah (Zedekiah) was appointed king to replace Jehoiachin.[2]

They lost their city and temple (2 Kings 24:18-25:21; 2 Chron. 36:11-21)

Jehoiakim had reigned for only three months when he was exiled to Babylon, but his successor Zedekiah ruled for eleven years. He pretended to submit to Babylon while at the same time courting Egypt and listening to the pro-Egypt leaders in the government of Judah (Ezek. 17:11-18). Zedekiah took an oath in the name of

the Lord that he would be faithful to the king of Babylon
(2 Chron. 36:13; Ezek. 17:11-14). He maintained diplomatic
contact with Babylon (Jer. 29:3) and even visited the court of
Nebuchadnezzar (Jer. 51:59), but he also sent envoys to Egypt to
seek the help of Pharaoh Hophra.

In 605, during the reign of Jehoiakim, the Babylonians had
deported some of Judah's best young men to Babylon to be
trained for official duty, among them Daniel and his three friends
(Dan. 1:1-2). The second deportation was in 597 (2 Kings 24:10-
16) when over ten thousand people were sent to Babylon. But
Zedekiah still favored getting help from Egypt, and in 588, the
political situation seemed just right for Zedekiah to revolt against
Babylon (2 Kings 24:20; 2 Chron. 36:13). Nebuchadnezzar
responded by marching his army to Jerusalem, but when the
Egyptian army moved to help King Zedekiah, the Babylonians
withdrew temporarily to face Egypt. Nebuchadnezzar knew it was
unwise to fight a war on two fronts. God sent Jeremiah to warn
Zedekiah that Nebuchadnezzar would return (Jer. 37), but
Zedekiah's faith was in Egypt, not in the Lord (Ezek. 17:11-21).
Zedekiah even called an "international conference" involving
Edom, Moab, Ammon, Tyre, and Sidon (Jer. 27), hoping that
these nations would work together to keep Babylon at bay.
However, Nebuchadnezzar stopped Egypt and then returned to
Jerusalem and the punishment of Zedekiah.

The siege of Jerusalem began on January 15, 588, and continued until July 18, 586, when the famine was so severe the people
were cooking and eating their own children (Lam. 4:9-10). The
invaders broke through the walls and took the city, looting and
destroying the houses and finally burning the city and the temple on August 14, 586. The Prophet Jeremiah had counseled
Zedekiah and his officers to surrender to Nebuchadnezzar and
thus save the city and the temple (Jer. 21; 38:1-6, 14-28), but
they refused to obey God's Word and had Jeremiah arrested as a
traitor! The officers put him under court guard and even dropped
him into an abandoned cistern where he would have died had he
not been rescued (Jer. 38:1-13). The hypocritical and weak

Zedekiah told Jeremiah to ask the Lord what he should do (Jer. 21), but the king refused to accept the prophet's answer. Zedekiah asked Jeremiah to pray for him (Jer. 37:1-3), but the king was a proud man who refused to humble himself and pray for himself (2 Chron. 36:12-13; 2 Chron. 7:14). When the Babylonian soldiers finally entered the city, King Zedekiah fled with his family and officers, but they were intercepted in the plains of Jericho and taken into custody. Jeremiah's prophecy had come true (Jer. 34:1-7; see also chapters 39 and 52). Zedekiah faced Nebuchadnezzar at his headquarters at Riblah where he was found guilty of rebellion and sentenced to be exiled to Babylon. But first, to give the king one last tormenting memory, the Babylonians killed his sons before his eyes—and then gouged out his eyes! Ezekiel in Babylon also prophesied that the king would attempt to escape and be captured and taken to Babylon, but he would not see the city (Ezek. 12:1-13). How could Zedekiah see the king of Babylon (Jer. 34:3) but not see the city of Babylon? The answer was: after he had seen the king, Zedekiah was blinded by his enemies.

After removing everything valuable from the city and the temple, on August 14, 586, the Babylonians finished breaking down the walls of the city and set fire to Jerusalem and the temple. The Babylonian officers captured the religious leaders of the city as well as the king's staff, the people who had opposed Jeremiah and given the king poor counsel, and had them slain before Nebuchadnezzar at Riblah. The priests had polluted God's house with idols and encouraged the people to break the covenant of God (2 Chron. 36:14; see Lam. 4:13 and Ezek. 8–9). The leaders of the nation had refused to listen to God's servants, so God sent judgment (2 Chron. 36:15-16). There was "no remedy" and the day of judgment had arrived. Only the poor people remained in the land (24:14; 25:12; Jer. 39:10; 40:7; 52:16) to take care of what was left of the vineyards and farms.

King Zedekiah lived in Babylon until his death and, in fulfillment of the Lord's promise through Jeremiah (Jer. 34:4-5), was given a state funeral. He certainly didn't deserve such an honor, but the Lord did it for the sake of David, the founder of the dynasty.

They lost their hope (2 Kings 25:22-36; Jer. 40–44)
The Babylonians treated the Prophet Jeremiah with exceptional kindness and gave him the option of going to Babylon or remaining in the land (Jer. 40:1-6). Like a true shepherd, he chose to remain with the people, even though for the most part they had rejected him and his ministry for forty years. His heart was broken when he saw the ruins of the city and the temple, but he knew that the Word of the Lord had been fulfilled (2 Chron. 36:21). The people had not allowed the land to enjoy the rest God commanded (Lev. 25:1-7; 26:32-35), so now it would have a seventy-year "Sabbath" (Jer. 25:11-12; 29:10-14; Dan. 9:1-3).

The Babylonians appointed Gedaliah governor of Judah. He was the grandson of godly Shaphan, who served under King Josiah, and the son of Ahikam, who faithfully supported Jeremiah (2 Kings 22:1-14; Jer. 26:24). Gedaliah assured the Jews who remained in the land that the Babylonians would treat them well if only they would co-operate, the same counsel Jeremiah had sent earlier to the Jewish exiles in Babylon (Jer. 29:1-9). Certainly the people knew the promise the Lord had given through Jeremiah, that the captivity would last seventy years and then the exiles would be allowed to return to Judah. God's purpose was to give them "a future and a hope" (Jer. 29:11), but they had to accept that promise by faith and live to please Him.

However, a group of insurgents led by Ishmael, who belonged to the royal family (2 Kings 25:25; Jer. 41:1), decided to usurp Gedaliah's authority. (See Jer. 40–41 for the details discussed below.) Several factors were involved in this vicious assassination plot. To begin with, Ishmael had designs on the throne and resented Gedaliah's appointment as governor and his submission to the Babylonians. (See James 4:1-6.) The army officers told Gedaliah that the king of the Ammonites had sent Ishmael to take over the land (Jer. 40:13-16),[3] but Gedaliah refused to believe them. Had Gedaliah listened to this sound advice and

THE END HAS COME

dealt sternly with Ishmael, things would have been different for the remnant in Judah, but he was too naïve to face facts. A third factor was the arrival in Judah of a large group of Jews who had fled to neighboring lands (Jer. 40:11-12). Their allegiance was questionable and perhaps they were too easily influenced by Ishmael. All the neighboring nations had suffered from Babylon's expansion and would have been happy to be set free.

Ishmael killed Gedaliah and took the people captive, but Johanan and the other officers rescued the captives. Ishmael and eight of his men fled to the Ammonites. Johanan became the new leader of the remnant and decided that they should all flee to Egypt rather than obey Jeremiah's message and stay in the land and serve the Babylonians. In a show of hypocritical piety, Johanan and the leaders asked Jeremiah to seek the mind of the Lord about the matter, and he agreed to do so. The Lord kept them waiting for ten days and during that time proved that He could keep them safe and well in their own land.

Jeremiah's message to the remnant (Jer. 42:7-22) was in three parts. First, he gave them God's promise that He would protect them and provide for them in their own land (vv. 7-12). Then he warned them that it was fatal to go to Egypt (vv. 13-18). The sword of the Lord could reach them in Egypt as well as in their own land. There could be no temporary residence in Egypt and then a return to Judah, for none of them would return. Finally, Jeremiah revealed the wickedness in their hearts that led them to lie to him and pretend to be seeking God's will (vv. 19-22). These leaders were like many people today who "seek the will of God" from various pastors and friends, always hoping that they will be told to do what they have already decided to do. The Jews rejected God's message and went to Egypt, taking the Prophet Jeremiah with them (Jer. 43:1-7).

However, the biblical record doesn't end on this bleak note but records the proclamation of Cyrus that the Jewish remnant could return to their own land and rebuild Jerusalem and the temple (2 Chron. 36:22-23). The Book of Ezra opens with this proclamation (Ezra 1:1-4) and tells the story of the remnant's

BE DISTINCT

return to the land. This decree was issued in 538 when Cyrus defeated Babylon and established the Persian empire. The Babylonians began their assault on Judah when their army invaded Judah in 606–05 and deported prisoners, among them Daniel and his friends. From 606 to 538 is approximately seventy years, the time period announced by Jeremiah (Jer. 25:11-12; 29:10). Some students prefer to start the count with the destruction of the temple in 586. Seventy years later would take us to 516–15, the year the second temple was dedicated and the captivity officially ended.

As they had so often done during their history, the Jewish leaders lived by scheming instead of by trusting the promises of God. Jeremiah had given the people hope by promising that God was with them and would see to it they were protected and returned to their land (Jer. 29:11). But the leaders abandoned all hope when they fled to Egypt, for there they died and were buried. How tragic that the faithful Prophet Jeremiah, who had suffered so much for the people and the Lord, should be buried in some forgotten place in Egypt.

As we come to the close of this record of the tragic decline and destruction of a great nation, we need to take some lessons to heart. *No nation rises any higher than its worship of God.* The nation of Israel was torn into two kingdoms because of the sins of Solomon who turned to idols in order to please his pagan wives. Because they worshiped idols and forsook the true God, the northern kingdom of Israel was taken captive by Assyria. It didn't take long for Judah to succumb and eventually be captured by Babylon. We become like the god we worship (Ps. 115:8), and if we refuse to worship the true and living God, we become as helpless as the idols that enthrall us.

The people who led Israel and Judah astray were conformers, weak people who followed the crowd and pleased the people. God warned them of their folly by raising up men and women who were distinctively different and sought to please the Lord, but these faithful witnesses were ignored, abused, and martyred.

The cynical playwright George Bernard Shaw defined martyr-
dom as "the only way in which a man can become famous without ability." He was wrong. People who have suffered and died for
the faith had the God-given abilities to trust Him, to put truth
and character ahead of lies and popularity, and to refuse to "go
with the flow" and be conformed to the world with its shallow-
ness and sin.

At this critical time in history, God is seeking dedicated, distinctive people—not cookie-cutter, carbon-copy Christians.
Friendship with the world is enmity with God (James 4:4) and to
love the world and trust it is to lose the love of the Father (1 John
2:15-17). We are to be "living sacrifices" for the Lord (Rom.
12:1-2), distinctive people whose lives and witness point to
Christ and shine like lights in the darkness. "A city that is set on
a hill cannot be hid" (Matt. 5:14). Faith is living without scheming. Start to explain away the clear teachings of the Bible about
obedience to the Lord and separation from sin, and you will soon
find yourself sliding gradually out of the light and into the shad-
ows and then into the darkness, eventually ending in shame and
defeat.

"He who does the will of God abides forever" (1 John 2:17,
NKJV).

NOTES

Preface and Chapter One
1. The book of 2 Chronicles parallels 2 Kings, and we shall consider it as we go along.

1. James and John had been with Elijah on the Mount of Transfiguration and wanted to imitate him by calling down fire from heaven on their "enemies." Jesus rebuked them (Luke 9:52-58). The Christian response to opposition is given in Matt. 5:38-48 and Rom. 12:14-21.

2. The inference here is that, after going to heaven, Elijah could do nothing further for Elisha. See Luke 16:19-26.

Chapter Two
1. Deut. 20:16-20 applied to Israel's attacks on cities in Canaan where the Jews would inherit the land. It was forbidden to cut down the fruit trees and thereby ruin their own inheritance. However, in foreign lands, their army could follow a "scorched earth" policy.

2. There's no indication that the events in this chapter are presented in chronological order.

3. Neh. 5:5 and 8, Isa. 1:17 and 23, and Amos 2:6 indicate that the Jewish people didn't always share God's love for the helpless widows. The early church had a special concern for widows that should be revived in the church today (1 Tim. 5:1-16; James 1:27).

4. The word is not "stool" as in KJV but "chair," and can be translated "chair of honor" or "throne."

5. Gehazi's part in this entire episode is most interesting (vv. 15, 25, 29, 36). It appears that Elisha preferred to have his servant be the go-between for him and the great woman.

6. Metropolitan Tabernacle Pulpit, vol. 25, p. 121.

Chapter Three
1. Joram seems to have had a pessimistic outlook on life and expressed it by jumping to conclusions. When they ran out of water, he didn't believe that Elisha could provide water for the three armies (3:10, 13). When he read the letter, he applied it to himself and totally ignored Elisha.

2. The water in the Abana (Amana) and Parphar came from the snow in the mountains around Damascus, so it was fresh and clean. Naaman had to learn that God's ways are above our ways (Isa. 55:8-9).

3. God also gave leprosy temporarily to Miriam because she criticized her brother Moses (Num. 12) and permanently to King Uzziah because he tried to be a priest (2 Chron. 26:16-21). Three sins must be avoided: covetousness,

malicious criticism, and rebelling against God's calling in our lives.

4. In 1 Cor. 9:1-14, Paul taught that the Christian laborer was worthy of his hire, and he included himself. But in vv. 15-27, he argued that he had the right to refuse their support for the sake of reaching more people with the Gospel. It was a personal conviction that he didn't impose on all the churches or all of God's servants. Paul knew that in Corinth especially, accepting money could put a barrier between him and the people he was trying to reach.

Chapter Four

1. "Ben Hadad" was the title or "throne name" of the Syrian rulers, just as Pharaoh was the title of the Egyptian king.

2. The NIV translates "doves' dung" as "a half a pint of seed pods."

3. Over a century ago, secular scholars used to smile at the mention of the Hittites and refer to them as "a mythological people mentioned only in the Bible." But excavations have revealed a powerful Hittite civilization that was frequently at enmity with Israel. Once again the archaeologists' spades have had to affirm the truth of Scriptural record.

4. It takes very little imagination to apply this scene to the church today. Jesus has won the victory over Satan and "this is a day of good news." Believers are enjoying all the blessing of the Christian life while a whole world is suffering and dying. How can we keep the good news to ourselves? If we do, we will answer for it when we face the Judge. How can we be silent in a day of good news?

Chapter Five

1. The Hebrew text simply says "do this great thing" (v. 13). The NIV reads "accomplish such a feat." The NLT reads, "How could a nobody like me ever accomplish such a great feat?" To a professional soldier, doing what Elisha described in v. 12 would be a "great thing." The issue wasn't what would be done by Hazael but how he would have the authority to do it.

2. This is the only mention of Elijah in 1 and 2 Chronicles. The Elijah in 1 Chron. 8:27 was a member of the tribe of Benjamin.

3. Along with David, the kings most often singled out for their godliness are Asa, Jehoshaphat, Joash, Hezekiah, and Josiah.

4. 2 Kings 8:24 says that Jehoram was buried "with his fathers," and this seems to contradict 2 Chron. 21:20. It's possible that Jehoram was originally buried in the tombs of the kings but that his body was later removed to another site. Popular opinion was so against honoring Jehoram that his corpse was removed from the royal tombs and placed elsewhere in Jerusalem.

5. Athaliah is always identified with Ahab but not with Jezebel. Although she learned much evil from Jezebel, we can't assume that Jezebel was her birth mother. "The daughter of Omri" (8:26, KJV) should read "the granddaughter

of Omri." See 2 Chron. 22:2, NIV.

6. The word "harlotries" or "whoredoms" in v. 22 refers to Jezebel's idolatrous worship of Baal. In the Old Testament prophets, adultery and prostitution were familiar images of idol-worship. Israel was married to the Lord when she accepted His covenant at Sinai and was warned to worship one God and not worship idols (Isa. 54:5; Jer. 3:14 and 31:32; Hos. 2:2). In the nation of Israel, just as adulteresses were stoned, so those who worshiped idols were slain (Deut. 13).

Chapter Six

1. Often in the account of salvation history, the future of God's plan rests with a baby or a child. Cain killed Abel, but God sent Seth as the next link in the chain. Abraham and Sarah waited twenty-five years for their son Isaac to be born, and baby Moses was supposed to be drowned but lived to grow up and deliver Israel from Egypt. During one of Israel's darkest hours, the Lord sent Samuel to Hannah and Elkanah. Now, the future of the messianic promise and the Davidic covenant rests with one little boy.

2. Jehoiada wouldn't allow the guards to kill Athaliah on the holy ground of the temple of Jehovah, but they could kill the priest of Baal before the very altar of Baal. Baal worship was a man-made religion and therefore a false religion. See John 4:22-23.

Chapter Seven

1. The Westminster Pulpit, vol. 8, p. 315.

2. Some believe that this was the man Jesus spoke about in Matt. 23:35 and Luke 11:51, but the text reads "son of Berechiah" (see Zech. 1:1). "From Abel [Genesis] to Zechariah [2 Chronicles]" would cover the entire Old Testament, since the Hebrew Bible ends with 2 Chronicles. Zechariah was a popular name among the Jews—there are twenty-seven found in the Bible—and it's not unlikely that more than one was stoned to death for his faith.

3. See 8:7-15; 10:32-33; 13:3, 22.

4. Many Jewish kings were assassinated. See 1 Kings 15:27; 16:8-10; 2 Kings 9:22-29; 15:10, 13-15, 25-26, 29-31.

Chapter Eight

1. The Decline and Fall of the Roman Empire, ch. 3. A decade before, Voltaire had written, "Indeed, history is nothing more than a tableau of crimes and misfortunes."

2. In numbering the rulers of Judah, I'm including wicked Queen Athaliah, who reigned for six years after the death of Ahaziah, and was Judah's seventh ruler. When young King Joash took the throne, Athaliah was slain.

3. Of the nine kings whose reigns are described in these chapters, five were assassinated: Amaziah (14:19-22), Zechariah (15:10), Shallum (15:14),

Pekahiah (15:25), and Pekah (15:30).

4. The phrase "as soon as the kingdom was confirmed" (14:5) suggests that, after his accession, Amaziah faced opposition and had to overcome it gradually. We commend him for waiting patiently to receive the authority he needed to bring judgment against the men who murdered his father.

5. The text suggests that the mercenaries first reported to their king in Samaria and then from there returned to the border country and attacked the cities. The king must have approved their plan or they wouldn't have returned to Judah to fight. Later, Amaziah tried to get revenge but failed miserably (25:17ff).

6. Note that the Prophet Jonah ministered in Israel at that time (14:25), and this fact helps us better understand his refusal to preach to the city of Nineveh. During Jeroboam's reign, the kingdom of Israel was proud, complacent, and very nationalistic. They were God's chosen people and they didn't want any other nation to interfere. Jonah would rather see the Assyrians destroyed by the Lord and refused at first to take God's message to them.

7. In those days, the soldiers often had to provide their own weapons and armor.

8. They are Asa, Jehoshaphat, Joash, Amaziah, Uzziah, Jotham, Hezekiah, and Josiah. Of course, at the top of the list is King David.

9. The phrase in v. 25 "with Argob and Arieh" has challenged students. The NIV and NLT translations suggests that these were two of Pekahiah's officers who were killed along with the king, while the KJV and NASB see them as two men who helped Pekah murder the king. The first interpretation seems to be the better of the two. Pekahiah was guarded by only two aides while Pekah had eighty men with him.

10. Pekah united with Rezin, king of Syria, in trying to force Ahaz, king of Judah, to join forces with them in opposing Assyria. It was out of this context that the famous messianic promise of Isa. 7:14 was born.

Chapter Nine

1. The dates for the reign of Ahaz are usually given as 732 to 716, sixteen years, but some scholars feel that these were the sixteen years of his sole reign as king. He was probably a vice-regent for nine years and a coregent with Jotham another four years.

2. This happens frequently in 2 Chronicles. See 11:2, 5; 15:1-8; 18:1ff; 25:7-9, 15-16; and 36:12. Prophetic ministry involves wisdom from God to understand the times and being able to apply the Word to the situation.

3. Keys to the Deeper Life (Christian Publications), p. 22.

4. No "Pharaoh So" is found in Egyptian history, but it's possible that "So" refers to the Egyptian capital city of Sais, which is "So" in Hebrew. Hoshea sent to So (Sais) to enlist the help of Pharaoh.

5. Perhaps Hoshea had to present himself in person to Shalmaneser, as Ahaz had done to Tiglath-pileser (16:10), and the king of Assyria wouldn't

allow him to return to Samaria. The government of Israel was very weak and the officers knew that the end was near.

6. In Col. 1:13, Paul used this military image: "translated us into the kingdom of his dear Son" (KJV). The word "translated" comes from a Greek word that means "to move a defeated population to another land." Jesus on the cross defeated sin, Satan, and death and the Father has transferred all who believe in His Son out of the kingdom of darkness and into the kingdom of life and light.

Chapter Ten

1. Most students believe that Judah was invaded twice by the Assyrian army, in 715 and in 701. The second invasion is given far more space in the biblical record because of the great miracle the Lord performed. It's difficult to see 2 Kings 18:7-16 as a part of the 701 invasion, but it was a prelude to it.

2. King Ahab turned to the wall and pouted because he didn't get his own way (1 Kings 21:4), but that wasn't the attitude of Hezekiah. Perhaps in looking toward the wall of his room he also looked toward the temple, which is what the Jews were supposed to do when they prayed (2 Chron. 6:21, 26, 29, 32, 34, 38).

3. J. W. Thirtle in his book Old Testament Problems (London: Morgan and Scott, 1916) proposed the theory that the fifteen "Songs of the Degrees (Ascents)" in the Book of Psalms (120–134) were compiled by Hezekiah to commemorate the fifteen extra years God gave him. Ten of these psalms are anonymous, while the other five are assigned to David (four psalms) and Solomon (one psalm). Thirtle believed that Hezekiah wrote the ten anonymous psalms to commemorate the shadow going back ten degrees on the stairway of Ahaz. After all, these are the "songs of the degrees." Since David was his hero, King Hezekiah must have tried his hand at writing psalms, and it's possible the Spirit of God gave him those ten psalms for that special collection.

4. Actually, when believers die, they leave the land of the dead (this world) and go to the land of the living (heaven)!

Chapter Eleven

1. Expositions of Holy Scripture (Baker, 1974), vol. 3 [2 Kings 8–Nehemiah], p. 244.

2. As you study the field commander's speech, it's tempting to believe that the Assyrians had someone in Jerusalem. The Rabshakeh not only knew about the Egyptian party, but he also knew that Hezekiah had removed the pagan altars (18:22), and that Isaiah had warned the people not to depend on horses and soldiers (18:23; Isa. 30:15-17).

3. The KJV calls him "king of Ethiopia," which refers to the region of the upper Nile. He was commander of the army at that time and eventually became ruler of Egypt.

4. Many great events in Jewish history were for the purpose of exalting Jehovah's name before all the nations. These include the Exodus (Ex. 9:16); the conquest of Canaan (Deut. 28:9-10); the entrance into Canaan (Josh. 4:23-24); the killing of Goliath (1 Sam. 17:46); and the building of the temple (1 Kings 8:42-43).

Chapter Twelve

1. Twilight of a Great Civilization (Crossway Books, 1988), p. 15.

2. God Tells the Man Who Cares (Christian Publications), p. 138.

3. If Manasseh was twelve years old in 697, then he was born in 709. He was coregent with his father from 697 to 687 and served alone for the next forty-five years. He was seven years old in 702 when his father had that severe illness, and he became coregent five years later (697). Since Manasseh was the heir to David's throne, his father surely taught him to obey the Word.

4. First and 2 Chronicles were probably written and circulated when the Jews were captives in Babylon, so the Holy Spirit led the writer to emphasize the messages the exiles needed to hear. If God could forgive and restore such a wicked man as Manasseh, could He not also forgive and restore His captive people? King Manasseh is a living witness to the truth of God's promise in 2 Chron. 7:14.

5. The emphasis in 2 Chronicles is on "all Israel," the uniting of the two kingdoms as the people of God. Many godly people from the Northern Kingdom had relocated to Judah so they would be under the spiritual leadership of God's Levitical priests in the temple dedicated to the Lord. The mention of Simeon in 34:6 reminds us that this tribe was politically a part of Judah (1 Chron. 4:24-43).

6. Some scholars claim that this whole episode was a "pious fraud" and that Hilkiah "found" the book in order to call Josiah's attention to the Law of Moses and the covenant Israel made with the Lord. But why would they take such a devious approach with a king who openly displayed his love for the Lord? Under the long reign of Manasseh, the law of God was ignored and openly disobeyed, and it wouldn't have been difficult for the temple copy of the Scriptures to be hidden for protection and then forgotten. However, this one scroll wasn't the last and only copy of God's law in the land, for the high priest and other temple officials certainly had copies. This was the opportune time for Josiah to hear the law of God, and the Lord arranged for it to happen.

7. There's no evidence that this Shallum was the uncle of Jeremiah (Jer. 32:7).

8. The Authorized Version of 2 Kings 23:29 says that Egypt "went up against the king of Assyria," when the Egyptians were actually assisting Assyria against the Babylonians. The NASB reads "Pharaoh Neco . . . went up to the king of Assyria."

Chapter Thirteen

1. Second Chron. 36:9 reads "eight years old," but the fact that he had wives (2 Kings 24:15) makes this very questionable, and it's unlikely that Nebuchadnezzar would appoint a young child to lead a vassal nation. After only a three months' reign, Jehoiachin was put in prison in Babylon (24:15), something the enemy wasn't likely to do to a child. Like ancient Latin, the Hebrew language uses the letters of the alphabet for numbers. The difference between eight and eighteen is the presence of a "hook" symbol over the letters for eighteen, and if the person who copied the manuscript failed to add the "hook," the error would be recorded and repeated. These occasional scribal errors in no way affect the inspiration of Scripture and do not touch upon any major teaching in the Bible.

2. The phrase "his father's brother" in 2 Kings 24:17 refers to Jehoiachin's father, Jehoiakim, whose brother was Mattaniah (Zedekiah) and therefore Jehoiachin's uncle. Zedekiah was the last king of the kingdom of Judah. Jeremiah's prophecy said that no son of Jehoiachin (Coniah) would occupy David's throne, and none ever did. After the exile, when the remnant returned to Judah to rebuild the temple, one of the leaders was Zerubbabel (Ezra 3:8; Hag. 1:1 and 2:20-23) who descended from Jehoiachin (Jeconiah) through Shealtiel (Matt. 1:11-12). However, though he came from David's line, he never sat on David's throne. Jeconiah never established a royal dynasty.

3. Perhaps the Ammonites hoped to restore the coalition described in Jer. 27 and revolt against Babylon. This, of course, would have been out of the will of God, but Ishmael would have jumped at the chance to become Judah's new leader.

Chapter One

1. What is the difference between a conformer and a trans-former?

2. Where did Ahaziah turn to get a prognosis for his health? Where should he have turned? Where or to whom do you turn when you are concerned about health issues?

3. When the two groups of soldiers and their captains were devoured by fire, what was the "dramatic message" from the Lord? How did the third captain avoid judgment by fire?

4. In the last judgment, who will be spared and who will experience God's vengeance in flaming fire?

5. For what three purposes might Elijah and Elisha have taken that last journey together?

6. What biblical examples show the benefits of joint ministry? Who ministers alongside you? If no one, why not?

7. What benefits can younger saints receive from senior saints?

8. What similarities can be seen between Moses and Elijah?

9. How can this statement strengthen you, "One with God is a majority"?

10. What were the three miracles of Elisha and the three corresponding spiritual messages for today?

Chapter Two

1. What does Wiersbe say that Elisha's miracles usually reveal?

2. Why did Elisha agree to help the 3 kings as they moved toward battle? Who was he really committed to helping? Why?

3. What did God promise to do for the 3 kings and their entourage? What did the Lord instruct the kings to do in return?

4. How was the attack against Moab an incomplete victory?

5. What does Wiersbe mean by the statement, "God often begins with what we already have"? What is it that you have that might become useful in the hand of the Lord?

6. What financial principles from the account of the widow's oil still apply to believers today?

7. What did the "unnamed woman" notice? What did she do about it? What excuses or obstacles might have held her back from caring for the Lord's servant?

8. Like the unnamed woman, how can you show hospitality to God's people?

9. What similarities are there between the accounts of Elijah and Elisha bringing a dead person back to life? What can be learned about God through these accounts?

10. What New Testament events echo the meal for the school of prophets? What truths are we reminded of when we meditate on the multiplying of food?

Chapter Three

1. What one mention does Elisha get in the New Testament? What was Jesus' point?

2. How did God use Naaman's slave girl to carry out the divine plan? What lesson can we take from this?

3. What parallels can be found between leprosy and sin? What parallels are there about the source of healing for both?

4. What had to happen to Naaman before he could be healed?

5. Why did Naaman become angry with Elisha? When have you felt angry with God for a similar reason?

6. How did Naaman respond after his healing?

7. What sin drew Gehazi on the path to judgment?

8. Where in the religious world today is God's work used as a "cloak of righteousness"? How could God's servants protect themselves from this temptation?

9. Why do you think "not greedy for money" is a qualification for elder?

10. What spiritual applications does Wiersbe make concerning the floating axhead? What is revealed about God's attributes in this incident?

Chapter Four

1. What five characteristics of God are revealed through Elisha to King Joram and his people?

2. Why did the king of Syria assume there was a traitor near him?

3. Why don't God's servants need to be afraid?

4. When his servant was afraid, what did Elisha pray for him? How can we pray to calm someone's fears?

5. Through what miracle did God show mercy on Elisha?

6. What did Elisha order to be done with the Syrian army? What effect did this have? In what conflict can you try this approach?

7. Which promises of God do you cling to the most?

8. What different effects does the Word have on a humble heart and on a proud heart? What examples of this do you remember from your own life?

9. In this account of famine and provision, what is revealed about the character of God?

10. What parallels does Wiersbe point to between the four lepers with the abandoned camp and the church?

Chapter Five

1. For what purpose did God use famines in the Old Testament? How, if at all, can we interpret the purpose of present day famines?

2. What does having the power to create or end famines reveal about God?

3. How would you explain the timing of Gehazi's story and the Shunamite woman walking in right then? When in your life have you seen God's timing?

4. How do you understand the relationship between providence and personal responsibility?

5. What do the events of the death of Queen Jezebel (and other wicked characters at that time) reveal about God?

6. God revealed to Elisha the power and violence in Hazael's future. In what circumstances would you like to know the future? Which things would you not want to know?

7. When we read the results of Jehoram's compromise with the world, what truth can we learn from his bad example?

8. What work did God want Jehu to accomplish? How did Jehu respond to this sudden opportunity?

9. Why did Jezebel mention Zimri to Jehu? How did Jehu respond?

10. How could Jezebel's gruesome death actually be God's will?

Chapter Six

1. What forces for good and evil were at work during the events of 2 Kings and are still at work today?

2. In Jehu's strategy to destroy Ahab's descendants, what was the first step?

3. How did Jehu absolve himself of guilt in the deaths of Ahab's 70 sons? Who did he infer was ultimately responsible?

4. In what way did Jehu go beyond his divine commission? What were some of the consequences of this?

5. In his desire and plan to rid the nation of Baal worshippers, what did Jehu fail to do? Why do you think this was so?

6. How did Jehu fail to follow the Lord with all his heart?

7. For what is Jehu mostly remembered? How could his legacy have been different?

8. How does seeking revenge usually turn out?

9. How did God preserve the messianic line when Athaliah determined to kill them all?

10. Jehoida and Jehosheba worked together for God's purposes. What couples in modern times have you heard of who worked together effectively for the Lord?

11. How does Wiersbe define revival?

Chapter Seven

1. What evidence have you seen that supports the principle "what a person believes ultimately determines how a person behaves"?

2. What three kinds of faith are exemplified by the three kings in this chapter?

3. What were the four stages in Joash's spiritual experience? What stages have you experienced in your own spiritual life?

4. What was the relationship between Jehoida and King Joash? What relational struggles might they have had?

5. When we make decisions about our church buildings, what balance should be remembered?

6. Why did King Joash so quickly abandon the faith after Jehoida died? How might this possibility have been prevented?

7. When did Jehoahaz show his "crisis faith"? How did the Lord respond? After the crisis was over, what happened to Jehozahaz's faith?

8. Why about Elisha on his death bed is an inspiration for senior saints?

9. What essential abilities, that King Jehoash lacked, are found in people "who live in the Word and walk by faith"?

10. What contemporary lesson does Wiersbe teach when comparing the ministries of Elisha and Elijah?

Chapter Eight

1. How did Amaziah begin his reign as King of Judah? What were his later sins?

2. Why was the forming of alliances a sin against the Lord? What alliances would be sinful today?

3. Why is it always better to seek the Lord before making a move or decision?

4. What incredible sin did King Amaziah commit after the Lord gave him the victory over the Edomites? What was his consequence?

5. When the Lord gives someone success, to what temptation are they vulnerable? How can the successful person stand firm in their faith?

6. Was the prosperity of this time in the life of Israel and Judah a sign of God's blessing for their obedience? How do you know? What does this tell us about the prosperity of our own nation?

7. What should we imitate about Uzziah's wise choice of Zechariah as counselor?

8. How did Uzziah go from success and blessing to rebellious sin?

9. Why did the priests have the courage to oppose King Uzziah's journey to the altar?

10. Do you have an "unholy ambition" in your heart? If so, what should you do?

Chapter Nine

1. In what two major ways was Ahaz a compromiser?

2. What three sins did the Israelite army commit against Judah?

3. How did the Israelites respond after the prophet's warning about their treatment of Judah?

4. How do you answer Wiersbe's question, "Does the Lord still chasten nations today as He did in ancient days?"

5. In what ways have you seen some modern churches imitating the world? In what ways have some churches remained faithful?

6. Why isn't the Lord pleased with just any sacrifice made to Him?

7. How did Urijah and his priests fail the Lord?

8. In what way did Hoshea go wrong?

9. What promises of judgment were fulfilled against the Israelites?

10. What are positive and negative examples of the principle that people become like the god they worship?

Chapter Ten

1. Who was Hezekiah's model and what was his overall desire?

2. What were Hezekiah's religious reforms?

3. Hezekiah began by cleansing the temple. In what way can we do a similar "cleansing"?

4. What united the people who celebrated the Passover with Hezekiah? What are barriers, then and now, to all God's people worshipping together?

5. How can we prepare our hearts to seek God?

6. As the worshippers left the celebration, how did they live out their rededicated faith?

7. Why did Hezekiah pay Sennacherib the tribute money? What other option(s) did he have?

8. How might you explain a direct prophecy of death that later the Lord, seemingly in response to prayer, changed? Is that change a possibility for other prophecies?

9. "I have heard your prayer, I have seen your tears." Who might need you to pass on these words of comfort from the Lord?

10. Why was Hezekiah so depressed about his life ending? What do Christians know that can take the sting out of death?

Chapter Eleven

1. How does Wiersbe describe Satan's pattern of attack?

2. Where do we see evidence of Hezekiah's struggle with pride? In what areas of your life do you struggle with pride?

3. When people admire our physical or material blessings, how can we respond in a way that avoids pride?

4. How had the Lord prepared Hezekiah for Assyria's assault against Jerusalem?

5. How can we have, as Wiersbe says, "the trials of life work for us and not against us"?

6. What did Hezekiah say to encourage the soldiers when they were threatened by the Assyrians?

7. What words does Satan use to frighten, confuse, or discourage believers? Through whom do these words come? How can we resist their effect?

8. How did the people of Judah respond to the field commander? When should we do the same?

9. "When the outlook is bleak," what does Wiersbe suggest?

10. What does this statement mean, "How foolish for the ax to boast against the woodsman"?

11. What NT Scriptures promise God's basic provision for our need? When have you seen Him fulfill this promise?

Chapter Twelve

1. Why is humility the key to God's blessing?

2. What can the facts of Manasseh's wickedness and his record length of kingly reign reveal to us about God's ways?

3. Why do you think Manasseh and his people ignored God's covenant and warning?

4. After Manasseh's awful wickedness, he called out to God in his distress and humbled himself. How did God respond? What hope can we gain from this?

5. What evidence is there that Manasseh's repentance was real?

6. What do you learn about Bible study methods after learning that 2 Kings makes no mention of Manasseh's repentance but 2 Chronicles 33 makes it clear?

7. How important was the leadership of the king for the condition of the country? What similarities are there with the church and its leaders?

8. As seen with Josiah, what can be determined by how someone responds to the Word of God?

9. What does the role of Huldah the Prophetess tell us about God's work through women?

10. What other times in Jewish history was there a renewing of the covenant? When would a corporate renewal of dedication to Christ be a good idea?

Chapter Thirteen

1. Why can it be said that the kingdom of Judah committed suicide?

2. What were the five steps (or losses) in Judah's decline into destruction?

3. If the Jewish people would have obeyed God's covenant, what difference would that have made in their lives?

4. Why was joining the idolatry of the other nations such a great temptation?

5. What was the final siege of Jerusalem like? When did it occur? Why did it occur?

6. What do we learn about God from the destruction of Jerusalem and the temple?

7. What was Gedaliah's big mistake as governor of Judah?

8. Why did Johanan and the leaders ask Jeremiah to seek the mind of God? How did they respond to the Word of the Lord? When have you "sought" the Lord while only being willing to accept one answer?

9. How do the key conformers and transformers during the time period of 2 Kings differ?

10. Who are "dedicated distinctive people"? Are you one of them?